GOD OF THE

GOD OF THE WILD PLACES

THE POWER OF ADVENTURE

Paul Yunus Pringle

With line drawings by Valerie Winter

 The Quilliam Press

First edition 2023
The Quilliam Press Ltd
14 St Paul's Road
Cambridge CB1 2EF

www.quilliampress.com

ISBN 978 1 872038 29 2

Printed in the United Kingdom by CPI Books

Contents

Have you ever felt stuck? Trapped? Were you assigned, or did you assign yourself a role, a station in life which now has you locked, inexorably, into a rut from which you cannot deviate? Did you make decisions based on your conditioning which now bind you to a path in life which appears fixed, immutable and limiting? Read on. I'll tell you why I did what I did. I'll tell you what I did and what changed.

Your passion, that which makes you feel truly alive, may be your salvation: the voice of the Beloved, calling you towards the life that is written for you.

Introduction

The sun began its descent behind the high dunes of Erg Mhazil.
I hauled myself to my feet, re-shouldered the burden of my heavy
pack which contained all I needed to survive this week, and left
Checkpoint Three. One of my bivouac-mates, a serving soldier,
army commando and veteran of the notoriously tough P-Company
selection had been forced to pull out at the second of today's mandatory checkpoints: the skin on his left foot was macerated and was
separating from the flesh. His injuries were the result of three days
and around 130 kilometres of running, walking and, occasionally,
crawling over dunes, dry wadi-beds and salt flats in temperatures
in excess of forty degrees centigrade. This was the Western Sahara,
in all its savage glory.

It made no sense that I was still there. Me! The 58 kg schoolteacher. The last few days had been among the toughest of my life and the thought of a further hundred kilometres was hard to contemplate. I was nauseous. My head pounded. Every square inch of my body ached and then, at the mid-point of the brutal 71 km overnight stage of the Marathon des Sables, I began the ascent into Erg Mhazil. The sky darkened, revealing the myriad desert stars. Soon I would be blind to their beauty in more ways than one. The light wind blurring the perfect crests of these 'Lawrence of Arabia' dunes hardly hinted at the hellish assault on mind, body and spirit that the night would bring. For years my heavy heart had pined for adventure. Soon I would be truly tested, forced to operate at the very limits of my endurance, from moment to agonizing moment, hour after glorious hour.

THE THEORY GOES like this: what a person wants to be when they are around nine or ten years old is, in fact, his or her destiny. Simplistic? Trite even? Maybe. I believe it holds a germ of truth regarding dreams and the desires of the heart, those things to which a child's spirit is so open and intimately acquainted. How many of the noble plans and chivalrous designs of childhood are either lost, trampled on, or perhaps consigned to the shadows of some understairs cupboard of the heart, only to be disturbed each time a chance comment or memory shines a torch into that forgotten place? So the dream, the connection to *wildness*, to the fierce joy of battles and dragons and comrades in arms, is lost, or sidelined, denied, suppressed or ignored … for a while, at least.

How many men in their thirties or forties or fifties are woken at 3AM by the neglected voice of longing or feel the ache for wildness screaming in their chest as they begin another soul-starving day in the office or factory, school or shop? The evening news feeds us with a diet of war in far off places, pandemics, violence in our streets and poisons in our food, and we remain afraid. The dreams of childhood are compromised as we are sucked into the lie that tells us that we must have more money, a bigger house, a faster car, better sex, and whatever else. We are told that being a good consumer and having all these things will protect us from what we perceive to be the chaos of the world outside. Our fortress of things becomes the criterion by which we measure our success and our worth. Many more of us slip, meaning well, into a life where there is only duty. Our motives may be fundamentally good, but we lose our connection with the vision. We become passive, numb, depressed. In either case our *wildness* is stifled and suppressed, and this natural impulse pushed into the shadows can become a brutal, vicious thing. So often men try to salve the pain of the loss of this childhood vision with alcohol, drugs, TV, empty sexual encounters, pornography, excessive work, gambling … the list goes on.

I have felt the longing for wildness that I speak of. A keening for something lost; a yearning cry from a place deep and ancient. I have glimpsed it often in the eyes of other men. I speak without apology of men in these pages. This is not to exclude or discount the experience of women, whom I love and respect. I write of men as a man. I feel as a man. Each day I struggle with and rejoice in the workings of a man's heart: my own heart. I offer women readers a glimpse into that world. It is my hope that you will leave knowing more of the hearts of men.

Men are wounded. We don't know what to do any more. The lines are blurred. There is nothing to define our role. Once, for better or worse, we looked to the world of work to define ourselves. Now women succeed and indeed excel in areas which were once perceived, albeit erroneously, as 'ours'. The necessary adjustments have been painful.

The district in which I grew up was a mining area. Now there are no miners. But a boy's struggle still starts early. Primary education grows ever more prescribed and regimented, with a spirit-crushing emphasis on targets and the perpetual assessment of the child against those targets. In this scenario the child seems to become little more than a unit for generating data. The high levels of stimulation required to grab and hold the attention of a boy at this age, combined with reduced opportunities for risk and physical activity brought about by a world perceived to be sinister and dangerous, can lead to him appearing 'difficult'. When such a boy is judged to have become too difficult, a label is often applied and medication employed to make him 'better'. These are, of course, generalisations and I do not for one moment minimise the struggle and discrimination which still faces girls growing up in our society, but that is not a story I am qualified to tell.

There is a cost, too, paid by the boy who does adapt, who does comply with the constricting role imposed on him. He learns the first lesson in an insidious syllabus which seeks to chip away at his soul and tell him that the wildness in his heart is bad. And yet it's not bad. It's beautiful. This wildness embeds the boy in the natural world; he is a part of it. For the sake of women as much as men, let us recognize that the much-discussed 'patriarchy' has damaged men too, as the overwhelming majority of men have had no stake in it. I make an assumption that what women want is healthy, safe men, who are connected to what is truly masculine. I use the word 'safe' in the sense of being rooted in that which is natural to an emotionally healthy, undamaged man: a hard-wired instinct to ensure the safety of women and children. The violent, abusive 'masculinity' paraded before us with ever-increasing prurience twenty-four hours a day by the entertainment media is a vile betrayal of authentic masculinity, a distortion further fuelled by the ongoing alienation of men and boys. I believe we are in error when we blame and denigrate masculinity *per se* for the ills enacted in the world by men. Our communities might be better served by a return to a truer, clearer vision of what authentic, protective, generative masculinity actually looks like.

Violent men are an appalling reality. In our woundedness and confusion, men cause the world to suffer. I believe that in our healing we can, and do, bring healing to the world. This book is about the reconnection to the healthily masculine wildness which I believe is essential to this healing. I pray that in these pages, men will see their own hearts reflected in such a way as to guide them towards genuine, connected brotherhood. Too many men walk through this world in isolation.

As humans our needs go beyond water, food and shelter. Many readers will have heard the story of the experiment ordered by Emperor Frederick II.[1] Determined in his grandiosity to prove that the tongue spoken in his land was the original language of mankind, he devised an experiment. He ordered his court scientists to take newborn infants and isolate them in a cave. His plan was to care for their every physical need but to deny them human contact. He intended to observe the 'natural' development of their language and thereby satisfy his ego. All the infants died. Our healthy development, indeed our very survival, requires more than the satisfaction of physical needs. We need human connection, to care and be cared for. Beyond this, even, we need to experience a degree of security, influence and belonging, of participation in our own destiny. We need to experience purpose and meaning in our lives. If we are to be whole, we must also experience challenge: a sense of being stretched towards our full potential. Disproportionate ease and comfort may even work against us, creating ideal conditions for the 'lower self' of the ego to take command, and setting up many obstacles on the path which leads toward the fulfilment of our real destiny.

The human mind has an extraordinary capacity for imagining alternative possibilities. When we connect with the vision that is our true heart's desire, and picture ourselves living that vision and vividly experience in our imagination what that

1 See J. Griffin and I. Tyrell, *Human Givens: A new approach to emotional health and clear thinking* (Chalvingdon: HG Publishing, 2007), p.105.

feels like, our creative subconscious will do everything in its power to align our reality with that vision. That's its job! On some level, we create what we believe to be true and move towards that which we focus our attention on. This book charts my journey from smallness toward fulfilment, and tries to show how I dared to climb out from under the weight of years of erroneous beliefs, acquired messages and harsh judgments, to accept and participate in a new vision of who I am and what is possible in my life. It also maps the voyage of a questing heart which finally came to rest in Islam. It's a simple book with a simple message: there is a beautiful wildness in the heart of every man. At some point life will call each of us to an adventure. This adventure will take many forms: a spiritual quest, a career change, the pursuit of a long-held dream or vision, the facing of loss or adversity, the launching-out on a voyage of recovery from addiction. There are as many forms to the adventure as there are adventurers. Yunus Emre has told us that in discovering the essence of life, 'souls take a thousand paths.'[2]

I can choose to accept or deny the call; each course of action has its consequences. If I accept the call and awaken from my numbness, there will be risk, trial and challenge. By risking the adventure and facing the challenge with intention, I may just connect with my higher purpose in living, my mission in the world. I can then return from the adventure with a gift which has the power to heal and invigorate both myself and others. This is the 'Hero's Journey' of myth, from *The Epic of Gilgamesh* to Star Wars. I will tell the story of how I responded to the persistent voice of longing and found my own way of

2 Yunus Emre, tr. P. Smith, as *The Turkish Dervish: Selected Poems* (New Humanity Books, 2012).

liberating a long-buried spirit of adventure by connecting it to my masculine heart.

I am not a scholar. I don't think my way through this adventure. I listen to the longing and allow it to return me to my soul's water, as the salmon returns to its origin. The story speaks not only of the soaring of the spirit. A man's journey to wholeness will, by necessity, lead him through the gateway of grief as he strikes his roots downwards, ever deeper into the rich clay of the masculine soul. This is the story of my own, long-over-due, initiation into manhood, a Vision Quest for meaning and higher purpose in my life. You may be familiar with the term 'mission' from the all-pervading company 'mission statements'. What I speak of is vastly deeper and richer than this; a way of encapsulating moments of revelation regarding my purpose for existing and distilling them into a phrase which can be held in my consciousness and used to invoke the power of intention.

Most men will never pick up such a book. If you have read this far, my guess is that you have also heard the longing voice. It would please me greatly if you enjoyed my story and laid it down afterwards with a certain sense of satisfaction. And if something here touches you and inspires you to strike out from the haven and risk the wild sea on your own voyage, then I wish you the joy of being in mission. I hope to nourish souls by showing glimpses of the God of the wild places.

XVI

CHAPTER 1

Jack at the Foot of the Beanstalk

A FEW SUMMERS back I found myself sitting at home, watching a TV interview featuring film producer David (now Lord) Putnam. The focus of the interview was a government teacher recruitment initiative. Putnam was paying tribute to one of his own schoolteachers: she had been the one who had made him realise and believe that he could make a good living from pursuing something he felt passionately about. He went on to say that as a result of this he had never really had a job, but rather a series of hobbies which had paid handsomely. Putnam was fortunate to have had this inspired guidance. My guess is that most of us aren't so lucky.

When I was a child in Scotland, around eight years old, I knew something. The dream was vivid and clear, vibrant, and as much a part of me as my hands and heart. I knew I was going to be a soldier. The games I played were all in preparation, like the mock hunting of a lion cub. I recall one long summer of industrial disputes when the grass was left uncut for months in the field adjacent to the council block in which I lived. For me as an eight-year-old, this was heaven-sent. That long grass became a jungle where camps were made, ambushes set and heroic battles fought. That same year my father took me to an open day at Dreghorn, the local army barracks. I remember so well the joy in my eight-year-old heart as I wandered wide-eyed among the tanks and howitzers, the excitement as I watched camouflaged soldiers abseil down walls and stage mock battles, complete with explosions and smoke. For a little boy with dreams of adventure it was a perfect summer.

What happened to that vision? I lost sight of the dream early on. Unlike Lord Putnam I never became aware that it was possible to pursue the dream. Instead I became afraid. I took onboard every fear and insecurity that passed close to me and added it to my own. By the time I was ten or eleven my view of myself had already begun to change, and the dream was beginning to crumble. Northern Ireland was in turmoil and the nightly news bulletins recounted the painful, tragic human cost as young life after young life, whether loyalist, republican, or British soldier, was destroyed. I began to feel ashamed of the dream I'd had as a young child. It all seemed so naïve and foolish in the face of such horror. I fumbled awkwardly into my teens and turned about-face, grew my hair and became a pacifist, opposed to all things martial in a wholesale rejection of my childhood vision. I turned my back on my fledgling dream. This was the beginning of many years of refusing the call to adventure, and my soul, by instalments, paid the price.

I repressed and denied the dream. I pushed it into the shadows where it became distorted. In the dark chamber of my heart I no longer felt like a hero. I felt like a coward. I had turned my back on the adventure. I had failed to prove myself in battle. Fear and shame formed a toxic seam in the bedrock of my sense of self and became the corrosive foundations of my life. My experience was one of isolation in an unfriendly, insecure world.[3] I sought safety in every action I took, every decision I made; and it was to be many years before I realised I could not, of myself, manufacture, or demand this safety from the world.

I drank; a sad substitute for true adventure and challenge. It took the edge off the fear and gave the illusion of safety. It muffled the nagging, insistent voice that tried to remind me of my vision. The voice became ever quieter as drinking became both a refusal of the call to adventure and a means of hiding from the shame I felt at my self-adjudged inadequacy and cowardice. I recall those times with great sadness. I spent my time in the Hebrides Bar, or wandering anonymously around a selection of bars in the centre of Edinburgh. I recall that it was on one of these peregrinations that I found myself, half drunk, walking aimlessly along George Street. It was autumn, and cold. It was evening and the sky was darkening: George Street was beginning to empty. I shuffled past the door of St Andrew's and St George's, looking up at the big, austere and firmly-closed church doors. I felt empty. My heart was heavy with a longing I didn't understand. I was in my early twenties living an existence that made no sense. So, I drank.

A movement just off to the left caught my attention. Between two epic-looking Corinthian pillars, up a couple of steps on the raised stone porch of the church, a man in his thirties, simply but elegantly dressed, was unrolling a little carpet. He carefully adjusted the carpet until it was lined up in accordance with some device in his hand. The orientation was southeast-ish, over in the direction of the North British Hotel and the beckoning mass of Arthur's Seat beyond. I stopped,

---

3 See Tom Cheetham, *Green Man, Earth Angel* (Albany: State University of New York Press, 2005).

leaned against the bus stop and sparked up an Embassy Regal, intrigued and trying not to be noticed. He put a little green skull cap on his head, took his shoes off and placed them neatly to the left of the carpet. Then he stood on the mat, raised his hands to his ears and folded them across his chest, right over left. He went through a beautiful, graceful set of movements: bowing, kneeling down, touching his nose and forehead to the carpet, then getting up again. I lost count of the number of times he did it, but there was a pattern. It was beautiful. I was mesmerised. He just didn't care what was happening around him. He was totally focused on something beyond. This was incomprehensible to me. He was ten feet away from me. I was in a desperate, meaningless limbo; he was touching paradise. I wanted to talk to him, but I was too ashamed. I stood at the bus stop smoking my cigarette, and watched him put on his shoes, roll up his little carpet and continue on his way. I wandered back along George Street in the same direction I'd just come from, down Hanover Street and into Leerie's Bar. It was dark in there, but warm and familiar. I pushed the man and his little carpet out of my mind, but he never left me alone after that evening. It was to be many decades before the significance of this event became apparent.

My focus turned ever more inward; I became more self-centred, more self-conscious, more afraid and more ashamed. I felt frightened and empty. I lurched from crisis to crisis doing the best I could. I was ashamed of my weakness and battled with a host of demons. The hearts of people close to me, people who loved me and whom I loved, were wounded, caught in the crossfire of an ugly, tragic dogfight. It was a contest I could never win. Alcohol had whispered a seductive story, promising to make everything better. It took a few more years of punishment and a lot of pain before my ego was subdued sufficient-ly for me to see through that lie. Alcohol had accelerated my decline into spiritual bankruptcy. Aged twenty-five, I accepted defeat and sought the help I needed to stop drinking.

I began to sort through the emotional wreckage I had cre-ated in my life. It was to be a long and difficult task. The self-absorbed concerns of my ego, with its petulant list of demands for unreasonable levels of safety, control and comfort, had bro-ken me. I had been compelled to take a hard look at myself and didn't much like what I saw. Ceasing to ingest a chemical on which I had become unhealthily dependent was uncomforta-ble to say the least. I felt as if I had been stripped of a layer of skin; raw, exposed, hyper-sensitive and often terrified. It soon became abundantly clear that the real challenge was not so much stopping drinking - I'd done that - but rather living with the feelings I experienced when I didn't have my 'anaesthetic' to damp them down. I was forced out of my stubborn, self-reliant, head in the sand way of living, in a sense 'blessed' by my defeated state. My way didn't work. I needed to find another.

I began to approach my life with a new spirit and resolved to make some sort of amends for my previous failings. The mist began to clear as months and years passed, and I started living with a new focus and purpose.

I learned much about life and people in the years that fol-lowed; about living in the moment and finding little pieces of joy in unexpected places. The removal of alcohol from my life had been essential if any progress was to be made. Drink had fuelled an approach to life dictated by the lower self of the ego, something so strong that hitting an emotional and psychologi-cal rock bottom had been required in order to break the cycle.

My mind grew clearer. But as time rolled on, however, slowly, imperceptibly, I lost any sense that life could be 'more'. I drifted, like so many men, into a resigned depression. I was merely killing time, getting through my life. I stayed too long in one place. Afraid to step into my life, I kept myself small. The longer I stayed put, the stronger became the gnawing feeling in my gut that I was somehow living someone else's life. It seemed that I was destined to struggle along unfulfilled, unhappy and directionless. I tried hard and feigned self-belief, but all the time a whole platoon of inner traitors plotted my inevitable downfall, and every creative spark was stillborn. Self-reliance didn't work. The world just seemed too threatening and complicated to deal with. I had often had the sense that the path I was trudging through life was the wrong one. Some sort of cosmic mistake had been made, a wrong turn taken somewhere along the way. Nothing felt or seemed right. Things went wrong. Everything was a struggle. It felt like my 'real' life was going on 'over there' somewhere, just out of reach. Sound familiar?

Every so often this feeling intensified as the path I was on intersected with another possible way, a different path. All of a sudden things flowed, life became natural, joyous, 'right'. This sense of rightness usually involved wild places. I felt it in mountains and forests. I'd felt it on an eight-day canoeing trip in Algonquin Provincial Park in Ontario. I'd connected with it many times in the Highlands of Scotland during my childhood. There was a sense of belonging and ease in the untamed wildness. I knew, intuitively, that these places held something profound for me; signs which spoke of what my life should be. But the meaning of those signs remained just out of reach.

Inevitably I'd lose my courage, or the 'different' path would become faint and obscure and I'd return to the old, 'safe' way and trudge on. I stumbled along this mistaken path in a kind of automated fog. Adventure, for me, became limited to the soulless scramble up the paperwork mountain. I descended, by increments, into a state of abject powerlessness, feeling victimized, weak and bitter, functioning in a depressed, robotic state.

I recognised my desperate need for healing but felt in my heart that it was beyond my power, often despairing of whether change was possible at all. Something bigger was needed, something beyond me, something of immense, transformative power. But even in my weak, defeated and doubting state I never gave up the search. I prayed to be released from the turmoil I was in. I had no clear idea as to whom or what I was praying. Desperation will do that. But the pain was such that I placed no conditions on my prayer. I had run out of answers.

Sometime in my mid-thirties I found myself sitting in an Indian restaurant. I was wearing a combat jacket, combat trousers and assault boots! In a rare moment of clarity I became aware (with not a little embarrassment) that I had never really let go of the childhood dream. In subsequent days I was assaulted by feelings of resentment, of having been cheated out of something: feelings of shame at a wasted life. The realization had come too late. I was too old for a military career, and anyway, underneath it all I had a sense that it wasn't really about that, it wasn't about being a soldier. The core of my childhood dream wasn't about guns and tanks. It was about adventure, courage, challenge, *wildness*. It was about my true nature as a man in the world. The childhood dream of being a soldier, the dream of adventure simply represented the first, tentative forays in the battle for purpose and meaning in my life; the battle for my soul. In retrospect I can also see the bigger picture, the whole long, painful, bloody campaign that took me from that immature, hero/soldier identity of those childhood summer days towards a different, more mature masculine way of being; a connection to the fierce, protector spirit of warriors of myth and legend, the warrior spirit of my ancestors in the border country of Scotland, the deep, transformative energy of the shamans who once walked the woods and forests of this island.

The shift from boy to man didn't happen spontaneously for me. It rarely does. I didn't know it then, but what my soul hungered for was initiation. Since ancient times it has been the job of the elders to contain and channel the rage of the boys and teach them the purpose of their fury. Their fury was needed to defend the village and protect the weak. It was the task of the elders to initiate, to bring the boys to a rooted, calm, secure state of mature masculinity, and for millennia the structures had been in place to do just that. For centuries in the West, however, we have been systematically dismantling those structures. Christianity, or rather, men speaking in the name of Christianity, sought to discredit the old gods, fearing for the souls of the flock. Christianity played an important role in lifting Europe out of much that was dark and brutal, but its theology has often been mistrusting of nature, 'depriving nature of the inner spirit which breathes through all things.'[4]

How different the history of our island, and indeed of the world, might have been if the early Celtic Christian church, more attuned to the earth and the old ways, had taken root. Or what might have been had we turned towards the deserts of Arabia, where Muhammad (peace and blessings be upon him): Prophet, Warrior, Leader, Lover, Friend, had brought a Revelation confirming the 'Primordial Revelation of the

4 Seyyed Hossein Nasr, *Man and Nature* (Chicago: Kazi Publications, 1997), p.55.

book of nature'[5] in all its terrible beauty. Instead the shamans were demonized along with the connection to the spirit world and the natural world which they represented. Cernunnos, the horned god of the pagan Celts, was distorted into the very personification of the devil. The Reformation further separated the people from the old ways and the old ideas of sacred space and ritual, citing idolatry and superstition. The 'Enlightenment' sounded the death knell and the old gods disappeared in a puff of reason. The Industrial Revolution riveted an iron tap over the trickle that remained of the sacred spring and re-routed it into an aqueduct high over the heads of the people. At the end of the nineteenth century Nietzsche declared that 'God is dead', and we live in a society that believes that he was right. This belief reduces us to cosmic insignificance with no purpose, no meaning and therefore no accountability.[6] It's as if mankind, in the West at least, in accepting what Nietzsche believed, is spiralling into collective nihilistic despair and madness. Yet it doesn't have to be like that. It is possible to change the direction we face. We can choose to tell ourselves a different story about what the world is like, who we are and what our place, our role, our purpose in that world is.

Maybe Cernunnos was indeed the devil. Perhaps the focus of the worship of the pagan Celts represented a perennial human yearning, a naïve and incomplete vision. While distorted, it may mirror something of the Source of creation; a faint reflection of something un-seeable. It seems clear that the shamans didn't hold a perfect truth, and the realms they trav-

5 Cheetham, p.25.
6 Henry Bayman, *The Station of No Station: Open Secrets of the Sufis* (Berkeley: North Atlantic Books, 2001).

elled in are dangerous. But something was lost with the passing of the old ways, and it was something that I needed. I was struggling to cope in an adult world with the wounded heart and psychology of a boy, vacillating between anger and fear. It would take something profound to launch me through the threshold into 'man psychology', a fierce fire to forge in me a man's heart. The sacred spring still trickled under the surface, and I could hear the faint babbling of its waters.

The helpers along the road to healing were many and varied. Each one took my hand and led me a little further along the path. Progress was slow and often faltering. A dear friend, Alan, and I talked long into many a winter's night of our experience as men in the world. I spoke of my struggle, my anger, my pain, my confusion. As I searched, I began to hear the same names cropping up in different contexts: Joseph Campbell, Robert Bly, Robert Moore, Douglas Gillette, Michael Meade, James Hillman.[7] I had a strong sense of being guided towards something. Many of these men wrote of initiation, and I began to recognise and identify the gnawing hunger which had been there for so long.[8] I started out in earnest to seek an authentic initiatory experience.

I set out on the journey from London to the New Forest in Hampshire with little idea of what to expect of a modern-day 'rites of passage' weekend. I had previously been sceptical about 'life changing' experiences but felt, at this stage, that I had little choice: something *had* to change. In true initiatory style, none of the men who had experienced the process I had

7 For instance Robert Moore and Douglas Gillette, *King, Warrior, Magician, Lover: Rediscovering the Archetypes of the Mature Masculine* (New York: Harper, 1991).

8 Michael Meade, *Men and the Water of Life: Initiation and the Tempering of Men* (San Francisco: Harper, 1993).

signed up for would tell me anything about it. They said they did not want to rob me of the power of the experience. They were right not to say too much and I will speak only of what I got from it for precisely the same reason.

Contemporary male 'Rites of Passage' experiences have come under much scrutiny since that time, with allegations of 'cult-like' techniques, 'brainwashing' and of being 'anti-woman'. This wasn't my experience at all, although it is certainly not for everyone. In many ways an organisation which seeks, specifically, to support men to step fully into mature masculinity, is out of step with the fluid gender identity politics of the day. I can only speak for myself. My experience that weekend was intense and, at times, quite scary; but I emerged more empowered and ready to step up to my responsibility and accountability as a man in the world, which included a mutually respectful, complementary relationship with women. I was made aware of follow-up courses, but I wasn't pressured to stay involved unless I chose to. In one weekend, my wounded heart was opened up wide, made clean and stitched back together. The healing could begin. I believe I was a better man for the experience.

I returned from that weekend genuinely transformed. I felt that I had reconnected as a man with the vital energy of my childhood vision. My fear had shrunk to its proper size and I no longer felt ashamed. My voyage over those days had followed the classic path of initiations from all times and places, the 'Hero's Journey'[9]: descent, separation from the mundane world and a shift into sacred space. It requires that an ordeal must be faced and special knowledge or 'secrets' acquired. The final phase is the 'return', a re-integration of the 'initiated man'

9 Joseph Campbell, *The Hero with a Thousand Faces* (London: Fontana, 1993).

into his society where he accepts his new responsibilities.

To 'initiate' means, literally, 'to begin something'. I felt a meaning and purpose in my life which I had never experienced before. Something was different. Something had begun, and I was ready to be of service in the world. The sacred spring had been opened up and flowed again; I'd touched my soul's water. I had expected to find something sensitive and fragile; instead I found a beautiful, protective ferocity. For the first time in my life I felt like a man. I had a mission in the world, and I gave words to that mission: 'I transform rage into blessing, creating a world of safety and healing.' I used it like a mantra and it brought much healing. It enabled me to release many of the demons I'd carried with me for years. I now knew the fury was there to bless and protect. It no longer ate me up inside.

For years I had taken all my sense of self and squeezed it into a box-file marked 'small.' I'd kept it on a metaphorical shelf between the one marked 'sensitive' and the one marked 'dependable.' Now here I was in my mid-thirties and, on the same shelf, I had discovered a great box-file marked 'Adventurer.' The trouble was that it had been empty since childhood. I'd spent years in the 'belly of the whale,' waiting for my life to begin, always looking for the 'easier' way, the path of least resistance. But now much of my fear and scepticism had been swept away. My life was more vital and colourful than it had been since the days of my childhood vision. I scented adventure on the breeze.

My first taste of such adventure was a husky-dog sledding trip in arctic Finland: eight glorious arctic winter days and nights spent skirting the Russian border through forested, snow-carpeted hills and across frozen lakes. I will never forget the sense of exhilaration and elation I felt as I released the slip-knotted rope with a sharp tug on that first morning. The six dogs in my team had been straining at the rope in their impatient desire to do what they were born to do: run all day in the cold, crisp snow. Their excitement was infectious as it rose to fever pitch. They barked and howled and leapt vertically in the air as they sensed the approach of our departure. These were not the fluffy, white, manicured huskies of Cruft's dog show. These beasts had dirty matted coats and faces crisscrossed with battle scars, but they were beautiful: tough, lean and with a power that belied their slight stature. They could run all day on a small bowl of watery food. At night each of them would turn in an ever-decreasing spiral, creating a small hollow in the snow. Here they would cover their noses with their tails and settle to sleep outside in -40C temperatures. In the morning they would emerge like zombies from the grave, pushing up through the snow which had buried them in the night. Around them I could see blood spatterings on the pristine snow, evidence of savage nocturnal disputes. They had retained a semi-wild quality, and when close to them, or when they looked directly into my eyes, I could sense, with a slight unease, the wolf that was still in their hearts.

I clung on to the sled as I tugged at the slip-knot which bound the straining sled and dog-team to a solid fir tree. The knot fell loose, the dogs lunged forward and the sled lurched after them, wood creaking, while I clung on for dear life. To my surprise I let out a whoop of joy as we sped through the magnificent snowbound landscape. I'm not given to such unbridled expressions of emotion but the feeling of liberation and euphoria were overwhelming. At last, this was my real life.

Day after day we travelled like this. The joy of moving with these animals never left me. We swept through forests which recalled half-remembered dreams of running free and breathing hard in such places. Time seemed different, frozen like everything else in that magical northern place. Periodically we would emerge from the forest and drop down onto the blinding white expanse of a frozen lake. These lakes sat slightly lower than the surrounding land and the air that collected there was of a penetrating cold. In one such place I allowed my eye to wander across the flat, featureless whiteness. I settled into the hypnotic motion of the sled and the precious solitude. I considered the harshness of the ice crust and the deep water lying beneath, waiting for the summer. I considered all the rage and turmoil that had existed inside me for so long and the deep lake of grief that lay beneath. Initiation had opened a gateway to that grief, but to reach it I'd had to smash through the ice wall which for years had claimed to be my protector.

We slept in wooden cabins in the forest, we fed and harnessed the dogs, we sweated in little wooden shack saunas. We were six very different people thrown together into this extraordinary experience. As often happens in these situations people shared more of themselves than one would reasonably expect of complete strangers. The majesty and wildness of the landscape coupled with the need to work as a team seemed to inspire an unusual level of trust. We spoke of loved ones, of illness and bereavement, of past mistakes and future adventures. We also laughed. In those small, stove-lit cabins in the depths of the Finnish forests I laughed more freely and heartily than I had done for years.

We stopped to eat one day in a clearing a few hundred metres from the invisible line that marked the Russian border. The sky was a bright azure, the air cold, clean and dry. The sun bounced ferociously off the brilliant snow and I had to squint to see the abrupt, dark tree-line of the border on the far side of a shallow bowl-shaped valley. I secured the sled and my dog team to a pine tree by the trail and made my way back along the track to where the guide was building a fire. I hoped the dogs would not eat their way through their harnesses as they had done on the previous two stops. As I walked, I saw distinctive tracks in the snow. I knew instinctively, what they were.

At the heart of my initiatory experience in the New Forest I had connected with a kind of protector spirit, a totem or power-er animal. I guess this is a metaphor, but the feeling of connection I felt at the time was powerful, visceral. It was part of me, the part that balanced me and provided the qualities I needed in order to be whole. I'd read about young men in tribal societies going into the wilderness on vision quests to contact their power animal. Before heading down to the New Forest on the momentous weekend of my own initiation I had been sceptical about such things to the point of being slightly embarrassed. But I had made a decision when I'd crossed the threshold into sacred space. I had chosen to surrender my cynicism and step into a world vastly richer and more abundant than the one in which I had existed until then. I had an intuitive sense that there was something beyond the world of empirical proofs and scientific method, beyond the insistent voices that said: 'this is all there is, let's measure it.' But the Christian worldview I had grown up with no longer satisfied. It seemed, with its emphasis on the 'fallen' state of humanity, somehow to reject the world. I felt, so deeply, that the world was not to be rejected. The wild places had something to teach me. Something which I had forgotten.

There before me on the trail were the distinctive broad prints of a wolverine: the solitary carnivore who spends his summers hunting and building up supplies to get him through the brutal winter months. This creature is the embodiment of tenacity, surviving in this harshest of environments, able to bring down a reindeer many times his size: a truly formidable creature. The prints seemed to my novice's eye to be recent: the breeze had not blown loose snow into them and they remained crisp and distinct. He was near, brother wolverine. The emotion I felt placing my hands in the prints took me by surprise; a deep, sweet joy coloured with the sadness of separation. Then the voice of Mikksu the guide called my name and I lifted my hands from the frozen snow to accept the steaming wooden mug of sweet tea which he thrust in my direction.

The sweetness of my near encounter with my totem animal was still with me as we arrived at our next camp with the slither and crunch of steel runners on snow, the creak of wooden sleds and the panting of tired, happy dogs. The darkness was alive with tiny ice crystals picked out like diamonds by our head-torches as we busied around the camp attending to the dogs and unpacking sleds. In the little shack sauna, I still held onto the feeling of a deep calm happiness, and I slept blissfully in the warm burrow of my arctic down sleeping bag.

Here in London, I look at the young men swaggering along inner-city streets with their pit-bull and Staffordshire terriers, and what I see is fear. I see these young men hide their shame deep in their hoodies. I see them draw a false strength from the fierce-looking dogs at their side, the same artificial security which some get from carrying a weapon. I see young men lost in a world without meaning, purpose, direction or hope. I see a transparent hunger for initiation, for a vision quest. What does the bull terrier represent if not the longing for connection with a power animal, a protector spirit, a guardian angel in animal form? It is the job of the elders to initiate the young, and it's not happening. 'If we don't initiate the young, they will burn down the village just to feel the warmth.' So goes the African proverb.

The village is burning.

CHAPTER 2

Crossing the Rubicon

INITIATION HAD REKINDLED a fire in my belly, a hunger for the Quest; but during the subsequent two years or so the call to adventure grew faint again, lost in the din of a chaotic world. Around me society seemed to move with ever-increasing momentum towards its own destruction. I watched as men and women bullied and schemed their way into positions of power, with no-one accountable for their actions and no-one accepting their responsibilities. In such a world the currency was fear. The strong exploited the weak. It was a world of interminable, infuriating automated call management systems, recorded and monitored 'phone calls, broken commitments, TV ad campaigns targeting toddlers: a world of people you couldn't trust, who seemed devoid of personal integrity. The only thing I felt confident about when dealing with such people was that they would try to rip me off.

I became increasingly convinced that the world was inhabited by people intent on bullying and abusing those weaker than themselves. Control and destroy was the name of the game. Ironically, in such a world the bullies, the exploiters, the abusers and destroyers were terrified too, victims of the state of fear and mistrust they themselves had created. Fear of losing power and privilege, and fear of not satisfying the insatiable lust for more. In such a world, men were fearful and suspicious of other men. There seemed to be too few true Kings to show us the way, too few true Warriors to defend the village and protect the weak. I felt that the nightmare had arrived. I struggled with the horrible feeling of being a victim, powerless to effect change, a sickening, debilitating impotence. At times I felt like a caged animal. I recall once watching a baboon in a zoo. The wretched creature's boredom and stress at its caged existence had mutated into a grotesque, self-harming anxiety causing the beast to pull habitually at its fur leaving raw, exposed patches of angry skin. I had lost connection with my vision and as a result had conjured up the 'reality' of a negative, hostile world. My focus had again turned inwards and it was convenient to place all of the darkness and blame 'out there'. I had lost the power of being a man of service in the world. It became clear that rather than projecting all of this out onto the world, I had to descend fully into it. I had to somehow quiet the petulant chattering of my ego. I needed a Vision Quest, a re-connection with my purpose, my mission, my reason for being here. I needed something tangible.

*

I felt good as I drove home, skirting Hyde Park. The awakening of springtime in the park mirrored my optimism. I had just attended a celebration honouring a group of men who had embarked upon a journey, the same road of initiation I had set out upon a couple of years previously. I understood its importance. Although it was not a physical journey in the accepted sense, I saw this very much as a waymarker on the voyage to the core of mature masculinity. I had attended many such celebrations and was again filled with a sense that the world was just a little bit better and just a little bit safer because of the step these men had taken.

I turned on the car radio just in time to catch a news bulletin. I was shaken by what I heard. The newsreader presented a catalogue of abuse and neglect inflicted upon an eight-year-old child, Victoria Climbié. Victoria had endured eighteen months of torment before dying at the hands of her aunt and her aunt's partner, to whom her care and education had been entrusted by her unsuspecting parents in Africa. This crime against innocence filled me with an impotent rage. The irony of my hearing of this tragedy just as I left the celebration was not lost on me. This outrage was a terrible manifestation of the crisis in mature masculinity I'd become so aware of. There had been nobody to defend the village. If we lived in a world where all energies were focussed on satisfying selfish wants, where power, control and greed swept aside accountability, duty and compassion, who would protect the vulnerable? I was overwhelmed by a profound sadness at the total absence of love, tenderness or safety in those last eighteen months of Victoria's short life. The impact of the emotion I felt was perhaps due, in part, to my having a child of the same age. I was aware of the vulnerability and the need for nurturing of children of this age as they try to make sense of the world and figure out their place in it, as they begin to dream. I doubt whether Victoria had had the luxury of dreams in those cold and lonely, fear-filled months. I had tears in my eyes as I drove through Paddington, past the hospital where my own child was born. When I arrived home I looked in on my daughter and kissed her on the forehead as she slept, the weight of the newsreader's words still pressing heavily in my chest.

I was horrified when I heard of the Climbié murder. Such crimes against innocence always horrify me. My past experience had been that after some days or weeks the horror began to fade and the outrage to subside as the mundane tasks of daily life and the distractions of the world pulled me back into a state of numbness. This didn't happen for me around Victoria's death. The sadness of it continually invaded my thoughts, even my dreams. I had an uncomfortable sense that, as an initiated man, I had to accept my duty to do something about it. But what? How could I transform the rage I felt at this crime into a blessing? That was what my mission called me to do. How was I to do it?

Even in an art-room packed full with the whole colour spectrum of paints, printing inks, pastels, card of all colours and flamboyant textiles there was a flat, grey wash which seemed to cover everything. Another day had passed. I had fulfilled the requirements of my job. The room was empty now. I clicked on the computer, in search of an adventure. I visited the Raid Gauloises website, revelling in the glamour of that most French of events, the original adventure race. My eye was drawn to an icon in the corner of the screen, a link to something called the 'Marathon des Sables'. I clicked on the icon, never dreaming of the scale of the adventure it would launch me upon. The rich golds, deep reds and burning yellows of the sandscapes shining out of the computer screen lit up the dreary room in which I'd endured the previous twelve years of my working life. The Marathon des Sables: a 130-mile, self-sufficient footrace across the Sahara desert. 'The toughest footrace on earth,' they said.

The dream of the desert shone vivid light and colour into my drab existence, casting all else into shadow. It was so powerful, so mesmerising. I knew in my heart that on some profound level this all had something to do with me, something to do with my 'real' life. This was it. This was what I had to do. I'd found it. I'd found the bridge over the chasm, the bridge that would connect me to the path I was meant to be travelling. This was the way to begin to fulfil my responsibility as an initiated man. I would finish this race. I would raise some money for the National Society for the Prevention of Cruelty to Children. It was that simple.

Joy welled up in me as I looked at the screen. It was so seductive, so romantic. It spoke to a place deep within me. Even the deep red-browns of the bloodied, bandaged feet of the 'day six' competitor drew me further in. It was irresistible. I had to be there among the vivid, lurid sponsors' logos and the impossibly deep, rich blue of the Berber headscarves.

That evening I called my father and told him what I intended to do. His words said that he was right behind me, but I detected a doubtful, concerned tone in his voice. I had never been a sporty kid. That had been the province of my brothers. I had been the quiet, bookish, 'clever' one. It was summertime in the early 'noughties', and tomorrow was General Election day. Late the following night my father sat up watching the election results come in. During a quiet spell he flipped over to the EuroSport channel. At the instant he changed channels, a documentary about the previous year's Marathon des Sables was beginning. It felt like a positive omen. I was on the path.

From that day forward my time was spent anticipating the end of working hours when I could return to the Marathon des Sables website. When the room was quiet again I would drift towards the computer, my hands still smooth, dry and powder-grey from kneading cold lumps of modelling clay. I'd tap in the address, the sequence now automatic to my fingers, and I'd step into the desert. I was barely aware of the flickering fluorescent strip-lights and the humming of the air-conditioner. How noisy that had seemed when first installed!

So it's late summer now. I'm pounding the pavements of Willesden Green. I carry a backpack full of heavy books (probably the best use some of them will ever be put to). I'm wearing ankle weights and I'm carrying a half-kilogramme dumb-bell in each hand. Other people running in the park look at me with a bemusement which is tinged, I judge, with just a hint of admiration. I feel good, I feel strong as I think back to my early runs of a month or two before. My lungs had burned and my legs had felt like lead. I remember the shame of those early runs, rising from somewhere deep inside, as I struggled to get as far as Queen's Park, a mile from my front door, knowing at the same time that I was registered for what was billed by some as 'The Toughest Footrace on Earth'. Now I run, and I chant to myself. 'MDS, MDS, MDS'. It feels good. Heroic. This is a strangely familiar feeling, like the feelings that welled up as a playing child engaged in some imaginary battle. I feel a certain smug self-satisfaction as I run past the newly-built, state of the art health-club with my heavy pack on my back. I can see them through the window, running on treadmills, watching TV screens. I feel connected to something beyond the ordinary, beyond the mundane. I guess I feel a bit special and for once I'm not ashamed of it.

The runs got longer and the pack heavier, and I continued with the chant when it got painful. I began to feel stronger and fitter than I had ever been in my life. One of my routes took me through parkland and up a road with a twelve percent gradient. The first time I 'hit the hill' it nearly killed me. I made it to the top but had to stop and fight for breath, doubled over, lungs, heart and legs screaming, the rusty taste of blood in my mouth. I was nauseous for five minutes before I could continue. Now I could do it five times in a loop with a full pack on my back before continuing on my route. This felt good. This felt very good. I had always been the smallest, the weakest, the last to be picked for the football team. This felt very good indeed.

CHAPTER 3

Battling with a Hydra

MY REGULAR WEEKEND training route took me from
Willesden Green in northwest London, down through the
busy streets of Kensal Rise towards Ladbroke Grove. Then I
would turn off the streets and onto the towpath of the Grand
Union canal. The canal had once been a vital artery carrying
the lifeblood of the city on coal, ash, cement and iron-filled
barges and narrowboats. It had since acquired an air of neglect
and decay and I would regularly see small teams of greasy rats
leaping from the water or scurrying across my path. Despite
the rats I still preferred the towpath to the fumes and bustle
of the London streets. I followed the canal all the way through
Portobello skirting the backstreets of the Notting Hill carnival
route, travelling in a vaguely easterly direction. The canal and
towpath grew less grubby and run-down as I progressed east-
ward, past the narrow boats of Little Venice and onto the Re-
gent's Canal, towards the ambassadorial mansions of Regents
Park and the animal smells of London Zoo. I came off the towpath before the busy market at Camden Lock and headed up
and over the pretty slopes of Primrose Hill with their dramatic
views over central London. The return stretch took me back

through the noisy streets and traffic fumes of Swiss Cottage and Kilburn to my home in Willesden Green. It was a distance of around twelve to fourteen miles, and I recall the sense of elation and achievement the first time I ran the whole route without stopping, carrying a full pack and with hand-weights. It felt great. I began to realise that once I pushed myself through my body's initial half-hour of rebellion it seemed that I could carry on indefinitely, albeit slowly.

It had all been a bit of a shock to my system to begin with. I had done little or no serious exercise since giving up on martial arts in my teens and now, in my late thirties, my body began to make its disapproval known. I had problems with back pain, severe pain in my knees, and shins and chronic blisters on my feet. All of these gripes began to settle down after a few weeks as my body grew accustomed to the greater demands being made of it, and it toughened up accordingly. I tried to get out for a run every day, even if only for four or five miles. Then at weekends I'd put in a couple of longer runs, steadily building the weight in my backpack. I felt some guilt at the amount of time this was taking up, which was time away from my family. There was, however, no alternative. I had to give myself the best possible chance of finishing the race, and that meant I would have to be in better shape than I'd ever been in my life. I had to put in the miles.

While my training was progressing well (if painfully), my fundraising efforts hadn't left the starting blocks. I must have written a hundred letters to any company I thought might be interested in having their logo displayed on international television. Nobody was interested, in spite of the fact that the race receives a good deal of media attention, especially in mainland Europe. 'Our charity budget has already been allocated for this financial year' was the standard response. Most didn't reply at all. One or two asked for further details only to lose interest when they realised I was a complete novice with no track record in such events. I wasn't going to win, so they didn't see why it would benefit them to get involved, regardless of the cause. I acquired a long list of charitable foundations and trusts from a friend and fired off another fifty or so letters, all to no avail. I just didn't seem to have the knack for fundraising.

I was starting to panic. It had been an anxious time sending off the first instalment of the entrance fee. It was an expensive race to take part in. Financial insecurity had always been a source of fear and anxiety for me. Even at times when I'd had more than enough money to get by on, I always felt that I needed just a little bit extra in reserve, just in case something went wrong. I always seemed to need that buffer of 'just a little bit extra ... in case ...' I'd been plagued by this fear of financial insecurity for as long as I could remember, going right back to worried conversations I'd overheard as a fearful, sensitive little boy concerning unexpectedly painful electricity bills. I had made a lot of judgements about myself with regard to finances. I compared myself to my contemporaries and I came out wanting. I had lacked vision around my financial life. I'd been excessively cautious and now I was paying the price. All the people I had grown up with had acquired mortgages and now lived in nice houses. I could have done this, but I feared making the commitment. Now, with the astronomical increases in London property values, I had missed my chance. I felt that I was destined to live in a rented flat forever and never to own my own place. I felt as though I'd failed my family. I would regularly beat myself up about all this, berating myself for my lack of courage and foresight.

This attitude had never changed anything, but had only served to keep me in the same place. It reinforced all my negative ideas about who I was and who I was going to be. It was part of the problem. If anything was going to change, I had to let go of this kind of thinking. This was not going to be easy, but I had reached the point of no return and had leapt over the edge when I sent off the first entrance fee cheque. My financial buffer was gone. This was a very uncomfortable feeling for me. There was a lot more expense to come and I had no idea how I was going to fund it. I could have supported the organiser's nominated charity (NOMA – Facing Africa). It was certainly a worthy charity, working for people in Africa with a dreadful facially-disfiguring disease. If I'd done that, the financial pressure would have been eased as I would get back half my entrance fee if I raised a certain amount in sponsorship. But it didn't seem right. Victoria Climbié had been the catalyst for the whole adventure, and was why I was doing it. My friend Felix told me that when I was in the middle of the desert, on my last legs, it would be the thought of Victoria that would remind me why I was there. He was right, of course. I had to follow my heart.

I never did get any corporate sponsorship. What I did get was the support – moral, practical and financial – of many good people, some of whom I had met through the men's personal development work I had done. I received a call from one such friend, Simon, one August evening.

'How are your fund-raising efforts going?'

'Progress is slow, to say the least.'

'When is the next instalment of the entrance fee due?'

'September.'

'How much?'

'Seven hundred pounds.'

'I would like to cover that for you.'

I was overwhelmed. He too had been touched by the Climbié case and wanted to do what he could. He also wanted to support me in my mission. I was blown away by this act of generosity.

This demonstration of individual kindness was not an isolated one, but it seemed to have a power which changed the course of events. Many men called me or spoke to me subsequently as word spread about what I was trying to do. Support was pledged, and soon a significant pot of money began to build up. This took the power from the bogeyman of fear who surrounded my own financial situation. It wasn't so bad. I found the money to buy the kit I needed and I paid the remainder of the entrance fee myself. I no longer had my emergency buffer of money, but I began to see that I didn't really need it. It was all about fear. All the money I raised could go straight to the NSPCC without being eroded by entrance fees and kit. It wasn't a huge amount of money – around £3,000 – but I was sure it would be put to good use. I knew it would help someone, even if only a little.

Perhaps more significant than the money raised was the ripple of positivity that had been set in motion. Something good was happening. Each time someone responded to what I was doing, some more goodness went out into the universe. I found myself firmly believing that each person who committed money to the charity or supported me in any way would be repaid ten-fold, if not financially, then by some form of joy coming into their lives. I think that's the way it works: whatever you put out into the universe will come back to you. Dave and

Jenny, who were colleagues at work, put together a fund-raising concert which brought together a normally-divided group of people.

So many people were generous. I could see the goodness in the world again, and that goodness was travelling around the universe, touching people as it went, all because of Victoria. There had been such an absence of the spirit of love or blessing at the end of her short life. I asked people to send such a blessing out to Victoria, wherever she was. I asked them to visualise holding her protectively and tenderly, providing the safety she had needed but not known. I'm sure the blessing reached her.

Best of Morocco sent details of mandatory kit, required medical documentation, sample training schedules and, of course, invoices. Best of Morocco were the official agents for the Marathon des Sables in the UK. I spent a lot of time visiting their website. It provided background information about the race, race diaries from previous years, training tips, answers to FAQs and some wonderfully gory photos of a runner's mangled feet from day six of a previous year's race. There was also much advice on medical issues, kit and nutrition. Once registered I was given a code to a runners-only password-protected area on the site. Here I could peruse the details of the other runners and exchange information and ideas about kit, training and so forth. I really felt part of something. The list of participants filled out as the weeks went by and more people registered. The runners came from all walks of life, from solicitors to charity workers, but I noted a strong representation from towns with military connections: Catterick, Aldershot, Hereford. This felt a little ironic given my childhood aspirations. One entry caught my eye. I think he was based in Aldershot: he was 6ft 3 inches tall, weighed fourteen stone and listed his occupation as 'paratrooper'. I scanned down the page to my own entry: London, 5ft 7 inches, 9 stone, occupation: 'teacher'. I felt a peculiar combination of embarrassment and amusement.

And all the time I ran the canal. I ran the parks. I ran the streets.

CHAPTER 4

The Road of Trials

Thames Meander: February 2002
Reading to London (Thames Ditton): 53 Miles

THE BEST OF MOROCCO website was a mixed blessing. The photos and stories from previous years' races were inspiring and the advice on kit, medical issues and jabs was really useful. And it all provided a tangible sense of community, of being a part of something. It was through the 'runners' forum' section of the site that I heard about the 'Thames Meander'. This is a training race exclusively for runners registered for the Marathon des Sables, or veterans of the desert race. It runs from Reading, in the county of Berkshire, to Thames Ditton, on the southwestern outskirts of London. The overall distance of fifty-three miles has to be covered within eighteen hours, and runners have to carry full desert kit (or the equivalent weight for those of us who had not yet acquired all the requisite paraphernalia). The idea is to replicate (as far as is possible in the UK in February!) the experience of the fifty-mile stage of the MDS. There was, however, a downside to being a part of this little virtual community. In the run-up to the Thames Meander I made the mistake of checking out a training schedule posted on the site by a fellow 'pilgrim'. It spoke of ankle weights, daily four-hour runs (6-8 hours daily at weekends), and trips to the seaside to run on sand. All the above were to be done, of course, with a heavily-weighted pack. It went on and on. I was horrified. When did these people sleep? Did they work? I immediately descended into fear and self-doubt. I wasn't covering half the weekly distances quoted in the schedule. I had been training hard (by my standards) for almost a year, but all positive feelings about my fitness seemed to evaporate as I scrolled down through the Herculean training programme.

But uncharacteristically this despondency didn't last long. My response was to up the weight in my backpack and the number of weekly training miles. I found myself looking forward to the Meander, despite the shock of reading other people's training schedules. (I wrongly figured that there was some exaggeration going on.) I'd be OK: I could do this. My capacity for pulling the wool over my own eyes staggers me still. The truth will out, however; and the 'outing', on this occasion, came in the form of the re-emergence of an old Achilles tendon injury, a hangover from my karate-obsessed youth. I'm sure it was largely psychosomatic, an outward manifestation of my fears; but it hurt like hell regardless.

The day of the race came around quickly. I had to get up early to catch the first Reading train out of Paddington station.

The tube ride to Paddington felt good. I had my backpack and all my gear and I felt quite heroic. I admit I did drift off into fantasy land, becoming the bold adventurer, the seasoned endurance athlete full of steely determination, the master of my own body. As I alighted from the tube at Paddington I was starting to believe that everything would be OK. I'd been training long and hard, by my own standards. I had received some physio and ultra-sound treatment on the Achilles injury, courtesy of a colleague in the physio department at work. I had it well strapped-up with elasticated bandages, and it felt fine.

The whole edifice began to crumble when I reached Paddington main-line station and set eyes on a couple of guys clearly heading for the same destination as me. They had all the same kit, as recommended on the website. The difference was that these guys were obviously the real deal. Proper athletes! They glowed with clear-skinned, conspicuous health and had physiques like thoroughbred racehorses. I felt my stature shrink. The fantasy hot-air balloon on which I had been drifting off had suddenly deflated and was crashing earthwards.

Things only got worse on the train to Reading. We had now been joined by several others (clearly from the same stable as the first two). The conversation soon got down to best marathon times, forty-mile training runs in the Yorkshire Dales and informed comparisons between various brands of heart-rate monitor, isotonic drinks and energy gels. I felt like a child and kept my mouth shut. At Reading station things deteriorated further. I found myself surrounded by implausibly fit-looking people stretching and pinning on race numbers with a practiced efficiency and a nonchalance that indicated that they had all done this many times before. I fumbled around with my safety pins like the complete novice I was. The last time I had worn a race number was in the 1973 Edinburgh Primary Schools Inter-Scholastic Games, aged nine (and Mrs Gallagher had pinned it on for me). I felt a familiar fear. This was not a fear of the race itself. It was a fear of being humiliated, of exposure as a fraud, a chancer. There, among the coffee shops and newsagents of the station I was struck (for the first time really) by the enormous reality of the task ahead. This wasn't a marathon: it was a double marathon. I had never even run in a half marathon. What the hell did I think I was doing?

'Are you the Para?' The gruff, Northern English accent comes from behind me. I turn to be faced by a big, powerfully-built man in his late forties. He doesn't look particularly fit, in the whippet-like sense that the others do. But he looks tough, as though he could pull a tractor from Reading to Thames Ditton. I catch myself wishing I could answer in the affirmative but smile ironically and say no. I can only put this case of mistaken identity down to a crew-cut and the olive-green wind-shirt I'm wearing, as I doubt the Parachute Regiment is bursting at the seams with men who have hovered around the nine-stone mark all their adult lives.

Mick (this is the big man's name) and I decide to start the race together. We all set off from Reading station at 9am bound for the Thames and the start line. We look like a little crocodile of infant schoolchildren, but instead of lunchboxes and school uniforms we've got full desert regalia, including fifteen-kilogram backpacks and chest-rigs with drink bottles. We pass through a deserted carpark and across a main road, much to the consternation of the garden-centre bound occupants of passing Volvo estates. We reach a rugby field by the river. Steve, the organiser of the race and an MDS veteran several times over, gives a final pep-talk and sends us on our way. It's an anti-climactic start. Everyone sets off walking self-consciously. No-body will run, afraid, in a very British way, of appearing arrogant or over-confident. There's an understated ripple of applause as one brave soul breaks into a deliberately measured run.

Mick had been a Para himself in his youth. We travel the first ten miles or so together. He has a big, raucous personality to match his physical stature. The miles pass quickly in his entertaining company. The weather is perfect; crisp and cold with a bright winter sun showing the archetypal English landscape off to advantage. Even the place names *en route* are so English: Henley, Marlow, Runnymede. We jog at a leisurely pace past boat-houses, house-boats, parkland, huge, stately-looking gardens and riverside mansions. This is all quite alien to me despite my twenty-plus years south of the border.

We're coming up to the ten-mile mark. Mick has waved me on. He's attending to a toe problem which has been causing him trouble in training. It has really been bothering him over the last few miles. I cross the river and draw in to the first checkpoint at Henley. I refill my water bottles, exchange a few good-natured words with the marshals (all MDS veterans), and continue on my way. The field has spread out considerably now and although I can see fellow 'meanderers' both ahead of me and behind me at some distance, I'm on my own.

I plod on, running for 15-20 minutes then walking for a while, then running again. My waist-rig, a glorified bum-bag, carries my water-bottles, some energy bars, dried pineapple and a Mars Bar. It's starting to irritate, bouncing uncomfortably against my thighs. I make a mental note to sort out a better system before the desert.

I'm approaching Marlow. I misread the directions on my route details and end up doing the scenic tour of 'little England' before eventually finding Checkpoint Two. I had been in the last third of the field anyway, but my lack of concentration has put me right towards the back.

I'm still alone and now I'm into a section of awkward, boring and very muddy riverside track. There is a series of gated fields, low and sodden with thick, clinging mud. I pass the occasional family group, out for a Saturday morning stroll with their (now filthy) dogs. I exchange a few words with an elderly gentleman in a tweed jacket, cap and walking stick, an 'old Major' type. He inquires what we're up to and seems unimpressed when I tell him. I don't think he's quite grasped the idea that the distance from Reading to Thames Ditton has to be covered today.

My spirits aren't so high now. I've been on my own for a good few hours. My hips, knees and feet hurt quite badly. The race rules dictate that everyone must carry a mobile 'phone (a safety measure as well as an organisational aid). I call a friend:

'Hi! How's it going?'

'Not so great. My feet hurt like hell and my hips are playing up. I feel pretty low at the moment.'

'How far have you got to go?'

This is not a good question to ask. I check my map against the route details and my heart sinks as the reality of my situation hits me hard. I reply in a half-laughing, half-despairing voice.

'Thirty-three miles.'

There is no joy in this experience now. It's become a sheer, bloody-minded slog. I will not give up. I cannot face the shame of returning tomorrow (my daughter's birthday) having failed. There is to be a party with plenty of friends and family in attendance. I can't fail; it really is not an option. But I've been on my own for many hours. I've long become accustomed to the 'Look! There's a nutter' expressions on the faces of passersby. I find myself wandering through places I just wouldn't normally be foolish enough to stray into alone. It's dark now: 10pm. I'm in the middle of Windsor Great Park with my head-torch on and rats scuttling around my feet. This is scary. I don't like it. All my city-born instincts tell me I shouldn't be here.

The physiological toll of my efforts is beginning to make itself known in ways other than the aches and pains I've been feeling for the past few hours. I've not been taking on board adequate fuel. I've been nibbling, but nowhere near enough fuel is getting into my system. The winter sun has long since gone in and the temperature has plummeted. The amount of energy I've been expending, combined with the fact that I'm not replacing it, means that as well as feeling physically exhausted I'm also very cold. Because I'm so cold, I haven't felt like drinking. I think I'm getting dehydrated. Yet I'm too low to care at the moment. I just keep going.

This is stupid. The whole race follows the river Thames. How the hell can I be lost? It's the middle of the night: I gave up looking at either map or directions hours ago and I'm very, very pissed off. When I came to Staines Bridge a few miles back I trudged on. I should have crossed the river at the bridge. Now here I am with a barbed wire fence blocking my way. The path just stops. This is a bloody nightmare. I make a forced detour through a council estate (in full desert kit!). This must have put about three, maybe four miles onto my race. I don't need this. I force myself on, swearing at the river. I feel like crying.

I endure the taunts of post-pub drunks as I try to thread my way through Staines to get back onto the river. I just keep going. I 'phone Steve P, just to speak to another human being.

I'm at the final checkpoint (about six miles from the scout hut which marks the finish and serves as a place to sleep until morning). I'm in the worst physical condition of my life. The ligaments in my hips are screaming their disapproval, the soles of my feet are bruised and battered (never in my life have they covered anything like this distance in one hit). My hamstrings feel like they are about to snap. It takes a massive act of will to raise my foot high enough to step up a kerb. I feel thoroughly dejected. Kathy (God bless her), one of the marshals, offers to lead the way to the hut which is some distance away from the river.

These final few miles seem interminable. I hurt so much with every step. I feel like weeping with joy as we round a suburban, tree-lined bend and see the tatty little scout hut. I am so utterly relieved. I stumble inside and collapse onto a bench. I eat some hot tomato soup and buttery bread. Then I eat some more soup, and more bread. I drink lots of tea. It's 2.40am. All the others are in their sleeping bags. I've come in dead last (not counting the ten or twelve who have dropped out). I drink some water and more milky, sweet tea and hobble to the toilet. My urine, what little there is of it, is a dark, rusty brown: I'm badly dehydrated. I drink more water and more tea. I struggle to drag off my trail-running shoes, then my double-layer wicking socks, then my blister-proof separate toe socks. I've trained for months without socks and I've been rubbing in surgical spirit for the past few weeks. The skin on my feet is like leather and I don't have any blisters. But my leg feels odd. A wave of anxiety wells up as I realise it's the leg with the elastic bandage. The instructions had been clear; six or seven hours maximum. I've been wearing this for in excess of seventeen hours. There is a neat indentation around the circumference of my shin, red and swollen on either side. It doesn't look pretty. But I'm too exhausted to care and crawl painfully, blissfully into my sleeping bag. I spend a fitful, feverish night and wake up in agony.

I peer out of my cocoon at the others gulping big mugs of coffee and devouring bowls of porridge and cereal at a long wooden table. I see the occasional limp, but no-one seems to be in as bad a state as me. I've seized up completely. In my crippled state, I'm forced to slide to the side of the hut and haul myself upright with the aid of a bench. It's excruciating. My hamstrings have seized and the backs of my knees have contracted into tight, knotted, painful balls. I can't walk, it's pathetic. A New Zealander, the winner of the race and new recordholder at nine and a half hours seeks me out and congratulates me on my 'awesome courage'. I'm touched by his self-effacing and generous spirit. He really means it. Steve singles me out for recognition for the 'gutsiest performance of the day' at the debrief. It appears that covering the distance alone, as I did, merits a special mention. I like that, but I feel like shit. Steve takes me to one side.

'If you can do what you did yesterday, you'll finish the desert race. I have no doubt. You've got what it takes.'

I want to believe him, but the way I feel, I can't echo his conviction. I'm in a great deal of physical pain, but far worse is the shame I feel at my physical condition. How did I ever have the audacity to think I belonged with these people? These are real athletes.

Mick is sweeping the scout-hut floor with a big broom he's found. The toe injury had ended his race at the ten-mile point. I'm impressed by his attitude. He's found a way of rising above his personal disappointment. He makes himself of service to other people. There's real dignity in that kind of humility.

I swallow my pride and beg a lift the five hundred metres

to Thames Ditton station. There is no way I can walk that far. Archie, a good friend, always generous with his time, is going to collect me. I sit for an hour on a bench by a bus stop seizing up even more. I watch the buses come and go and worry that one of the skateboarding kids will run into my aching legs.

Archie can't believe the shape I'm in. He helps me into the car the way I've seen him help his elderly mother into his car. My swollen and indented leg has not returned to its normal shape or size. The little canyon created by my negligent use of the elastic bandage is still perfectly formed.

The initial reaction to my hobbling, crippled entrance to the birthday party was one of nervous hilarity from all present. To be fair, they had no frame of reference for what I had just experienced and I guess I must have presented a fairly comical figure. After the obligatory greetings and a big (and painful) happy-birthday cuddle, I retreated to my bed. It felt very good indeed, womb-like in my bruised and shattered state.

With a spectacular lack of foresight, I had arranged to drive to Edinburgh (my home town) the following day. But the human body has an extraordinary capacity to heal itself. By the next morning, although still in great pain, I had repaired enough to make the journey. The day after our arrival in Scotland my mindset had changed from one of 'I can't do this' to one of 'If I'm going to do this I'd better ratchet up the training'. I headed for the Pentland Hills just outside of Edinburgh with my backpack, and put in a good ten-miler, up and over the gorse and heather-covered slopes. It felt like a scene from Mel Gibson's *Braveheart*. Being there on the summit, looking out over the breathtaking skyline of my beautiful city: the castle, the craggy outline of Arthur's Seat, the Forth Estuary and the Kingdom of Fife beyond, was an uplifting feeling. To the South

I could see the border country, the land of my ancestors: those wild border raiders. I connected all of this with the satisfaction of being able to get to this place three days after completing the Thames Meander and felt a ferocious joy. Oh, yes. This was good.

CHAPTER 5

In my Ancestors' Footsteps

I REMEMBER ANOTHER of those regular visits to my home town of Edinburgh, maybe ten years before. It was summer, and the sun was shining. The Edinburgh Festival was in full swing. It was a good place to be and I felt the sweet sadness of nostalgia as I wandered through the familiar streets of the Old Town, past the Heart of Midlothian, St Giles Cathedral and the City Chambers. The reassuring dark mass of Edinburgh Castle loomed behind me, watching over my shoulder as it seems to do wherever in the world I find myself. The crowds grew denser as I walked down the Royal Mile, passing kilted pipers and tourists and actors and jugglers and fire-eaters and street performers of every description, with endless fliers thrust into my hand at every turn. It all got too much after a while, and drawing on my local knowledge I slipped down a narrow Old Town close and away from the crowds. Tucked away in the mediaeval back-streets off the Royal Mile I discovered a tiny music shop specialising in traditional folk instruments. I was lured inside by intriguing glimpses of musical gems hidden in the semi-darkness within. My eyes settled on a curious and apparently haphazard collection of wood, leather, brass and velvet. Rarely had I seen such an instrument and never at close quarters. It was a beautifully-crafted set of Scottish smallpipes. The smallpipes are a quiet, sweet-sounding, bellows-blown bagpipe originating in the border country which straddles Scotland and England, related but very different in character to their more famous (and more strident) Highland cousin. I knew from scraps of conversation on the subject with my father, that my surname is a Border name, but I'd never really thought much more about it. But when I picked up those pipes, something changed. I connected with something very powerful. I connected with a sense of ancestry, of identity, of belonging. This feeling of connection happened at a physical, visceral level. I knew I would own and play a set of those pipes one day.

The discovery of the smallpipes started me on another journey, a journey towards the roots of my identity. The Pringles, I discovered, had been a powerful border clan, famed and feared during the infamous era of the Border Reivers. The Reivers were ruthless bands of armed horsemen who terrorized the region on either side of the Scottish/English border in the sixteenth and early seventeenth centuries. The hairs on the back of my neck stood up and a dark pride swelled in my chest when I discovered this 16th century quote in a book about the Reivers:

> The country dare not kill such thieves for fear of feud
> … If they be but foot loons and men of no esteem …
> it may pass unavenged, but if he is of a surname, as a
> Davyson, a Young, a Burn, a Pringle or a Hall … then
> he who killed or took him is sure himself, and all his
> friends (especially those of his name) is like, dearly to

buy it, for they will have his life, or of two or three of his nearest kinsmen, in revenge."[10]

In the dark month of 'Black November' the Reivers would launch raids across the border, killing any man who opposed them, stealing sheep, cattle and horses, and taking hostages for ransom. The words 'blackmail' and 'bereavement' are their only legacy to the English language. Yet there was a kind of honour amongst them. Women and children were not physically harmed and truces were, by and large, respected. The symbols of Scottish culture that I'd grown up with: tartan and kilts, Bonnie Prince Charlie, the '45 rebellion and the clans of the Gaelic North, were mostly drawn from Highland culture. That is a beautiful culture, a rich and wonderful thing, but it isn't really mine. I don't have a Highland name. My roots are not in the Highlands. Discovering a warrior heritage of my own was a powerful revelation. I bought my smallpipes and began to learn and play the music of the borders, my music.

This stuff is important. There is something primal about music which touches a very ancient place inside me. Music that is connected to the land has an even greater power. Take the most sophisticated, modern city dweller, and put him in a social context such as a wedding, and you can bet it'll be the passion and ferocity of the jigs, reels, polkas and bourées that will fire him up, or the calypsos and African polyrhythms, that will get him dancing. Even if he manages to contain himself, you can be sure that his heart beats a little faster when he hears the songs of his people and his land. I know that's how it gets me, although I've never been much given to dancing. I can

---

10 G.M. Fraser, *The Steel Bonnets: The Story of the Anglo-Scottish Border Reivers* (London: Harper Collins, 1989).

sometimes feel it in the authentic music of other lands and other people. I am exhilarated by the music of North Africa, the music of the oud and the duduk. I am deeply moved by the ancient music of Ethiopia played by Alemu Aga on the 'Harp of King David'. Indian ragas performed by Lakshmi Shankar or Hariprasad Chaurasia touch me profoundly. The inner 'soulscape' which the unmistakeable authenticity of this music connects me to is a land that is home to all people. There is no flag planted there.

Certain music also serves to soothe the soul. But therein lies the dilemma. Music, precisely because of its primal power, has to be treated with care, especially a music detached from any sense of the sacred. I am grateful that I had long since turned away from the path of alcohol before the advent of the rave scene in the UK, a scene I might otherwise have become involved in. My sensitivity to music would, I judge, have made me a sitting target for trance music, with its intense, hypnotic beat. I have no doubt in my mind that my defences against the spell cast by such music would have been easily breached, setting in motion a kind of gravitational downward pull with regard to my behaviour and attitudes. I'm also appalled and dismayed by the nihilism, violence and misogyny which spews out in the lyrics of some contemporary 'musical' forms. Ears and minds seem to have become desensitised to this. So, while I think music can be a force for good, even for healing, at its best reflecting something of the harmonies which exist in the natural world, not all music is equal. I find myself increasingly selective with regard to the music I expose myself to. I know how vulnerable I am to its charms.

It was during this period of my life, following a series of 'chance' conversations and introductions, that I found myself sitting in Cricklewood Mosque in London. It was late on a Saturday evening. The upstairs room of the mosque was full. I had no understanding of what was happening, but it appeared that prayers and litanies were being recited, led by Sheikh Babikir Ahmed. Sheikh Babikir would later show me much kindness and guidance. I watched entranced as the atmosphere of heart-felt devotion built up. The repetitive chanting (I later understood this as *dhikr*, or 'remembrance of Allah') was accompanied by ever more focused rhythmic movement. This was not empty dance or empty 'music'. It was clear to me, even then, that here was something intimately connected to the sacred. Both *dhikr* and *hadra* (the sacred movement) were 'orchestrated' by the Sheikh. And the central importance of his direction was not lost on me.

'Going it alone in spiritual matters is dangerous.'[11]

'You need a skilful guide; you cannot start this ocean-voyage with blindness in your heart.'[12]

True guidance in matters spiritual is, for me, essential. My perceptions are often unreliable. If I listen to my own ideas without seeking the counsel of an appropriate spiritual adviser, I have the potential to get myself into all sorts of trouble. In his beautiful book *Signs on the Horizons* Michael Sugich writes eloquently about the intoxicating power of the *hadra*, a power which demands strict spiritual courtesy of those who participate. The power of the *hadra* must be guided and con-

11   Alcoholics Anonymous World Services, 12 *Steps and 12 Traditions* (York: AA General Service Office, 1960), p.60.

12   Attar, Farid Ud-Din, *The Conference of the Birds*, ed. and trans. Afkham Darbandi and Dick Davis (London: Penguin, 2011).

tained by the Sheikh.[13] I was not Muslim when I found myself in the midst of that *hadra* in Cricklewood. I was not permitted to take a full and active part, but something deep within me longed to. It was an intense first exposure to Islam and one which I now view as a privilege. Something was placed in my heart that evening.

During that trip to Scotland I rooted around, finding out as much as I could about my Border heritage. I came across the Pringle clan crest. *Amicitia Reddit Honores* read the motto: 'Friendship Brings Honour'. Above it, in the centre of the crest, was a scallop shell. The scallop shell, I knew, had been the sign of the pilgrim since the great mediaeval pilgrimages to Santiago de Compostela on the Atlantic coast of northwest Spain. 'Saint James of the Starry Field', as it translates, was famed as the resting-place of the bones of Saint James the Apostle, and pilgrims from all over Europe had travelled a route via the great mediaeval cathedrals all the way to what was then considered the third most sacred site in Christendom, following Jerusalem and Rome. When the pilgrims arrived at Santiago, after a journey of many months on foot, they would make their way to the Atlantic Ocean and pick up scallop shells from the foaming surf as a sign that they had made the pilgrimage. To this day the 'Camino', the pilgrim route to Santiago, is waymarked with the sign of the scallop shell. My ancestors, it seemed, knew the power of sacred journeys. But it's never that simple. 'St James of the Starry Field' is known by another, less palatable name: Santiago Matamoros, St James the Moor-slayer. Make of that what you will.

I am drawn to sacred places. I have made a number of

13 Michael Sugich, *Signs on the Horizons: Meetings with Men of Knowledge and Illumination* (Michael Sugich, 2013).

journeys to holy sites, often with a partly-formed spiritual intention. These were, in a real sense, pilgrimages. Sometimes the journeys had the energy of devotion, sometimes of reparation or atonement, but more often a sense of the search for purpose or healing. One such journey was to Jerusalem. At every turn there I was faced with iconic images of the faith I grew up with and which had shaped me to a large extent. Around every corner I found myself stepping into the locations of great and momentous events I'd heard tell of since infancy: the Via Dolorosa, the Garden of Gethsemane, the Mount of Olives. But Jerusalem, for me, was not exclusive. Yes, the Holy Sepulchre felt sacred, but I also felt the power of the 'Wailing Wall', and most powerfully, which surprised me at the time, on the Haram Al Sharif; The Noble Sanctuary, and the Masjid Al Aqsa; 'The Farthest Mosque' located there. But that is a whole other journey, and a different book.

To me, on that first visit, Jerusalem felt like the 'navel of the world', the Omphalos. There was inherent power in the place itself, but I was also aware of the power generated by my own intention in being there. On some level I had made the journey sacred by my intention.

I believe any journey, indeed any positive action, can be made sacred when it is done consciously, with sacred intent. When I was a wee boy my mother called this 'offering things up to God'. Ordinary, everyday things, from homework to drawing a picture to tidying my room, even a grazed knee could be 'offered up' and made sacred by that action. Now, all these years later I smile a warm smile at the simple beauty and wisdom of it.

To walk, to keep moving, is in my blood and in my bones. Some people think it's crazy that I'd rather walk or run a few miles than take the Tube or jump on a bus. But I hate to be closed in. When I'm stressed or worried or anxious I run, or I walk. The repetitive motion seems to work like a mantra, to clear my mind and centre me, calming the torrent of thoughts and feelings.

Laurence Freeman, a Benedictine monk who has written extensively on the process of meditating using a repeated word or mantra, describes this process as 'the pilgrimage of the heart'.

I can push this theory a little further. I have often been drawn to the idea of meditation, acutely aware of my need for an anchor in the sea of noise and anxiety which is modern life. I have repeatedly embarked with absolute sincerity and resolve on the pursuit of a contemplative discipline only to find my focus drifting after a few dedicated weeks or months, unable to quiet my busy mind. I seem to need the complete physical absorption of distance running, or walking in the hills, to cut through the noise and impose a benevolent dictatorship of stillness. A dark shadow is lurking in the wings when I take this apparently noble pursuit to the extreme: an element of avoidance, of self-punishment even. Sometimes I run or walk or climb because it's all I can do. Nothing else makes sense. The world becomes too absurd and confusing. The simplicity of the journey from A to B, however painful, offers an escape from that world. The pain of the endurance race becomes a shelter from the pain of everyday life.

It's a sweet paradox that continuous, repetitive movement can take me to a place of great stillness and peace. It enables me to let go of what is unimportant and reconnects me to what is sacred. It's a natural thing, a primal thing. When my own child was very small, picking her up and walking with her was the only way to soothe her crying, the only way to calm the tiny person's outrage at having been so rudely ejected from her blissful, warm, protected state of unity with her mother into the noisy, insecure duality and apparent separateness of the world. The repetitive, rocking movement and the closeness to the walking adult had the power to take her back to that state of blissful connection.

Sometimes I feel like I'm not so far from the ancient nomadic roots of humankind, when life and travels were dictated by the ripening of different food-plants, the movement of the prey-beasts and the vagaries of the weather. The need to be on the move is still there, rooted deep within me. When I look at the caravans of the gypsies and travellers I sometimes glimpse something in the shadows, deep inside me, something akin to envy, a vague memory of something lost, something my ancestors knew about.

One of my ancestors, Robert Henry Graham Pringle, is buried in the Sahara. He was killed a few short weeks before the German surrender in North Africa during the Second World War. He was 31. I remember seeing the occasional photograph of him when I was a child, but he only became a real person to me when I was around eighteen. I was home on holiday from college, rummaging around in the understairs cupboard for some documents I needed. I stumbled across a little bundle of papers relating to my father's father, Robert Henry Graham Pringle. I looked at a photo. I looked at his shattered watch. I looked at his army paybook with its details of his height, his weight, his age, the colour of his eyes, the tattoos on his arms. I looked at the official telegram informing my Nana of his death, complete with its rubber-stamped King's signature. I pictured her in her twenties, watching the postman walk towards the door. I tried to imagine her dread, but I couldn't begin to. In the space of a few seconds this man whom I'd heard about now and again, became a real person, an important person, my Grandfather, my blood.

Now Robert Henry Graham Pringle lies in the sands of Tunisia, the sands of the Great Sahara. Trooper Robert Henry Graham Pringle of the Lothian and Border Horse: a tank regiment. D.G. Antonio records the actual incident in which my grandfather and five of his comrades died.

> Stukas were spotted at breakfast-time and our crews waited in their tanks in unhappy anticipation. The familiar circling of the silver-grey machines above their chosen target took place to our rear. The sudden swoop of the leader followed by the rest was directed at our echelon. There came the long unnerving rumble of bombs and then the uncanny silence which the fading noise of the departed bomber only gradually penetrates. A tank and an ammunition lorry were destroyed and six lives lost.[14]

It is with a combination of pride and loss that I think of his last days in the heat and dust of that magical, terrible place. He died a warrior, fighting for a vision of freedom.

---

14   D.G. Antonio, *'Driver Advance!': being a short account of the 2nd Lothians and Border Horse, 1939-1946* (Edinburgh: Lothian and Border Regimental Association, 1947).

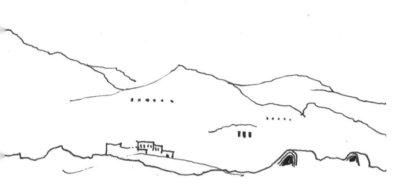

CHAPTER 6

The Crucible of the Desert

WITH THE EXCEPTION of a couple of film crews who would be covering the race, the charter flight from London Gatwick to Ouarzazate in southern Morocco was to be filled exclusively with Marathon des Sables participants. I whiled away the time spent pre-flight in the departure lounge spotting the desert-bound lunatics amongst others bound for Malaga, Florida, or wherever else normal people fly to. It felt good and somehow heroic to be a part of it all as I boarded the plane with my fellow 'pilgrims'. I spent the flight sitting next to a Parachute Regiment P.T. instructor (the guy from the B.O.M. web-site), and it did little for my already fragile faith in my fitness for the task ahead. He was a big man. His solid, muscular frame filled the whole airline seat and I had to crane my neck to see past him and out of the window.

As the aircraft lifted up over the jagged, snow-capped spine of the Atlas Mountains I was astonished to be able to watch the shift into a different climatic system. The northern slopes of the mountains were carpeted with green vegetation, an extension of the fertile green plains below. The grey clouds beneath our left wing seemed to billow back on themselves when they reached the spine-like apex of the mountains, forced to retreat northwards by some invisible, repelling force. Beyond the ridge, the skies were of an unbroken azure, the earth beneath parched and yellow. The suddenness and drama of the change were breathtaking and I knew that the world I would soon touch down in would be very different from the one I had left. As the aeroplane began its descent, so began the descent in my psyche. All familiarity had been left behind, leaving in its place the disequilibrium from which springs all change. But before I could claim this change in my life, I had to face the ordeal which lay ahead. It began to feel like an adventure: the next cycle of my initiation.

The casualness and informality of the smiling customs officials at Ouarzazate airport was in stark contrast to their post 9/11 counterparts in Gatwick. Security had been tight and the baggage checks thorough. Booking information from the organizers had warned of the penalties for attempting to carry even apparently innocuous materials such as cooking fuel. No such rigour with our uniformed friend in this desert airport, who waved us through with a smile and a declaration of 'I theenk you err all crazy, yes?' Paradoxically Ouarzazate smelled of wet sand. They still appeared to be building most of the town. It looked as if that's the way it had been for some time. The only people I saw on the 15-minute bus ride from the airport to the somehow unexpectedly well-appointed Berbère

Palace hotel were two groups of boys and the occasional pair of men. The first group was bathing in some sort of shallow concrete canal, the second playing football on the most lethal looking gravel pitch I have ever seen. Ominously, the men sat in the shade.

The Berbère Palace had been commandeered by the organizers, Atlantide Internationale, and had been given over to the UK contingent. With rooms allocated and gear dumped, most of us had gathered in the large courtyard by the pool. This was a pleasant place to be: the dappled shade of scattered parasols, the silver glint of sun on the pool, the blue and white mosaic floor undulating beneath, and above, everywhere above, the deep blue of the desert sky. The adobe walls of the hotel sheltered us on four sides. They were a rich red, with straw still poking out in patches. Almost everyone drank from litre bottles of mineral water. The paranoia about remaining adequately hydrated had begun during the flight and showed no signs of abating.

I was billeted with Ian Archer whom I had met on the Gatwick Express *en route* to the airport. We had recognized each other as fellow MDS participants immediately, despite never having met. It's hard to say why, exactly. Ian was a mild-mannered schoolmaster who seemed to be enjoying his conscious downshift to being a small-town postman. He was fast approaching fifty but you could see that he was in good shape, a veteran of many marathons and several ultras. We joined Mick (from the Thames Meander) in the courtyard and he introduced us to the others at his table: Tom, Sandy, Terry, and Barry. These guys were all serving soldiers, with the exception of Terry, who was a police colleague of Mick's but also ex-army. We spent the afternoon drinking our water and laughing at Mick's apparently limitless supply of outrageous anecdotes from his years in the Parachute Regiment. I was happy and relaxed in the company of men.

The following day, as we wound our way high into the mountains, the road clung precariously to the side of sheer, crumbling cliffs. Although the road was barely wide enough for our coach, the driver launched us around blind bends with terrifying abandon. At one heart-stopping stage he managed to get the outer tyre on the double-tyred back wheel out over the edge of the cliff, the inner tyre left scrabbling desperately for purchase, our driver oblivious to the whole drama.

The aforementioned paranoia about hydration had led to most of us consuming our generous allocation of Sidi Harazem mineral water with a cavalier disregard for the inevitable consequences. We were now several hours into our journey and suffering the combined agonies of fifty-plus distended bladders. Our dauntless driver was sticking steadfastly to his schedule, regardless of our desperate protestations. He was determined to stay with the other two coaches (whose passengers, it soon became apparent, were in the same condition as we were).

The pre-ordained (and oh! so welcome) lunch stop eventually arrived and saw a maniacal exodus from all three coaches followed by the spontaneous formation of a neat horseshoe shape as around a hundred and fifty men simultaneously emptied their over-stretched bladders. The women, who made up around a quarter of our party, made alternative arrangements on the far side of the coaches. I swear there was an audible sigh of mass relief.

It was baffling. We had been driving through the desert for hours. The last sign of life had been a crumbling adobe village about forty minutes before, yet no sooner had I opened the brown paper lunch bag provided by the organization and surveyed the tinned fruit, biscuits, nuts and raisins, paté and a little cake, than a small horde of children appeared out of the desert.

They were dressed in ragged western clothing circa 1982, (down to and including patterned polyester sweaters). They were barefoot and smiling with hands outstretched. I wasn't hungry and handed over most of the contents of my paper bag. A couple of minutes later they were gone, scurrying across the sand with armfuls of booty and delighted expressions on their faces.

Things are different here. On my way back to the coach I carelessly scratched my leg on a thorny bush. By the time we reached the limit of the coach's journey into the Sahara, about an hour later, the superficial scratches were already inflamed, angry and infected. I was glad of the alcohol wipes and iodine spray I had brought with me as I cleaned up my legs by the side of the road.

As I stood in the sun I pondered the recent twists on my journey to this place. Five weeks prior to the race I'd received an e-mail from a researcher at Granada Television. They were making a documentary about the desert race, looking in particular at the effect such an event has on the human body. They wanted three or four people to follow through the race. The British agents for the race had given Granada the e-mail addresses of all the UK participants. I replied, registering an interest, and forgot about it. A few days later I got a call from Jo, the Granada researcher who had put out the initial e-mail message. She asked me about the race; my reasons for participating, my fears and expectations. We talked on the 'phone for half an hour or so and my unorthodox ramblings about vision quests and mission must have been unusual enough to merit further investigation, as after a couple of days Jo and a producer/director called Gemma came down from Manchester to talk to me at home. They asked more questions and took some video footage to see how I came across on screen. Everything seemed to go quite well. Jo called to tell me I was on board, and the adventure took on another dimension.

I was sent details of preliminary tests and filming to be done at Qinetiq, a research establishment in the South of England, based on a site previously owned by the Ministry of Defence. This was scheduled for two weeks before the race.

Qinetiq was very James Bond: all uniformed receptionists, security tags and men in white coats with clipboards. I was introduced to Shona, the last of the chosen four (I had met Ronnie and Alan at Waterloo station earlier that morning). We were led into a slightly intimidating boardroom for a briefing from Marty, a sports physiologist and scientific advisor for the documentary.

He talked us through the programme for the day. First, we had to swallow a radio pill. This technology had been developed by NASA to monitor astronauts whilst they were in space. The James Bond quotient jumped another notch. The pills would record core body temperature readings every sixty seconds and send the data to a receiver carried on a waist belt. The data could later be downloaded to a computer for analysis. We would be swallowing one of these each morning during the race so that Scientist Marty could monitor what was happening to our bodies as the days progressed. I felt slightly odd swallowing all that micro-technology, which recalled childhood memories of a film about a miniaturized submarine floating around inside a human body.

The first test was designed to establish a maximum heart-rate measurement for each of us. We donned heart-rate monitors and did a shuttle run to exhaustion, with the time allowed for each leg of the shuttle denoted by a shrill electronic beep diminishing as the test progressed. This was followed by body mass index tests. My ludicrously low body fat figures were a source of great amusement. The afternoon tests were designed to look at how much fluid we were losing under exertion. We were all accurately weighed (with and without clothes, heart-rate monitors, water bottles and shoes), then escorted to an environment control chamber (the Bond factor had by now gone completely off the scale). The chamber was set to Sahara conditions: very low humidity, forty degrees Celsius and full solar load. The heat hit me like a slap in the face as I entered the chamber and a film of sweat formed instantly on my forehead. I climbed onto the treadmill. We ran for three ten-minute sessions on the treadmill, the speed increasing each time. I felt good. I felt strong, my heart rate stayed satisfyingly low and my core body temperature remained stable. This was all good news. I stepped off the treadmill, everything was weighed again and plenty of clever calculations were done. I didn't really understand what was going on, but I was having a great time. It was all very exciting and different. I was loving the whole experience.

Now we watched our coach as it trundled off along the main Trans-Sahara trunk road, having reached a point where even our indomitable driver could go no further. All three coaches had disgorged their loads of bodies and kit and there we stood in the middle of the Sahara Desert: 150+ souls and a neat row of suitcases and backpacks. The suitcases in particular looked incongruous. They would be collected and returned to the

Berbère Palace once the two-day acclimatization period was over and we entered the self-sufficient phase.

The next stage of the journey to the bivouac was on the back of an open lorry supplied by the Moroccan army. Big Mick clambered onto the truck in a manner which spoke of familiarity with such things and held out his hand to pull me aboard. The combination of his considerable bulk and my considerable lack of bulk almost launched me the two miles to the bivouac without the aid of a truck. We bounced off the tarmac and into the desert. I felt a surge of elation as the adventure really started. The leaf springs of the huge and aged truck groaned as we lurched and bounced across trackless desert. It felt like a scene from the WW2 desert movie *Ice Cold in Alex*. I stood on my little case in an attempt to see over the high slatted sides of the truck. It was magical. There I was, in the heart of an adventure, not just dreaming about it. I could feel my heart pumping the sheer joy of it around my body.

The bivouac sat in a dusty bowl surrounded by low mountains or jebels. The French were already there in numbers and the bivouac was alive and pulsating. The 'real' runners were still training even at this late stage, an intimidating sight as they ran by like native gazelles, apparently unimpeded by the loose rocks and cloying sand. To the north of the bivouac a rocky jebel teemed with ant-like competitors, all trying to get a signal on their mobile 'phones. Camp was strictly divided. To our left lay a media 'village' of stiff starchy canvas wall tents, gleaming white in the Saharan sun and off-limits for competitors on pain of disqualification. To our immediate right stood the commissaire's control tent, the communications point and the ominous 'Doc Trotters' medical tent. This was where many of the gory photographs on the website had been taken. Beyond both of these lay the 'bivouac concurrents', the competitors' bivouac, a motley horseshoe of moth-eaten 'tents'. These tents were black hessian sacks sewn together and stretched haphazardly over a couple of rough wooden poles and loosely anchored in the sand with wooden pegs. Tent allocation was a free-for-all. Big Mick called me into Tent 58, which was to be my home for the next week or so. Each tent housed nine people. Tent 58 contained Tom, Harry, Sandy, Terry, Mick, Ian, Joe, Barry and me. Soldiers, ex-soldiers, an ex-marine, a merchant banker, a postman and myself. The language was rough and there were many stories of dubious exploits in far-flung places, and yet these were good people. My regard for them was to grow as the event progressed. We were a peculiar combination, but one that seemed to work.

The night passed with sleep punctuated by trips into the darkness to relieve my overworked bladder. I fumbled around in a disorganized backpack trying to locate a head-torch, followed by further fumblings for flip-flops. The soldiers didn't seem to fumble for anything. Their packs (or bergens as they referred to them) seemed to magically offer up the required piece of kit as soon as they were opened.

We spent the next day attending to the various formalities: the ditching of the suitcases, registration, medical checks (an ECG printout must be supplied along with a medical certificate), checks on mandatory kit items (antivenom pump, compass, head gear, sunglasses etc), a food check (mandatory minimum 2000 calories per day), allocation of salt tablets and distress flares. It was a tedious and at times frustrating day with long queues in the baking sun and many problems trying to communicate with French-speaking officials. I was glad when it was over. But these were all minor irritations.

My fear of people and my social awkwardness had evaporated. I belonged in Tent 58. I was a part of something. I was accepted. I was at home and at ease, and I was happy, genuinely happy. All my usual self-doubt and mistrust of my body and its capabilities seemed to be swept aside by the sheer joy of being there. We lined up for the last of the meals supplied by the organization. I opted for the Boeuf Bourguignon. Only the French could produce such an excellent meal in the middle of the Sahara. You just had to admire their style. As I wandered around with my tray trying to locate my tent-mates, something caught my eye. The man squatting at a low table, eating with his hands was dressed all in blue, a beautifully rich shade of blue. He wore a long, loose robe of an expensive fabric and his head was covered with the head-dress of a desert nomad. He reminded me of Omar Sharif in *Lawrence of Arabia*. His limbs were lean and finely muscled. His features were also fine. This was Lahcen Ahansal, a Moroccan runner and the winner of this race for several years in succession. He had a palpable aura around him. I couldn't help staring.

I took my little ration of a half-bottle of red wine and donated it to big Mick who was celebrating his 48th birthday. Self-sufficiency was to begin the next day. After dinner I returned to Tent 58 and looked at my bergen. 15 kg with water, 13 kg without. Weight had been another great obsession in previous months. I'd weighed and re-weighed every item. All but the essential had been discarded. The smallest, lightest example of every item of kit had been selected, cost permitting. I had even found myself cutting the corners from foil-wrapped food packets and sawing my toothbrush in half to save weight. It was crucial to get the contents of my pack and their weight right. Now it was right and it was beautifully simple. Everything I needed was in that small pack. Everything that mattered was on my back. It was liberating, a good feeling. As I shouldered this burden, I shed the baggage of everyday life.

Stage 1: Oued Draa - Oued Mird. 26 km.

The high-pitched yodelling of the Berber bivouac teams shatters the desert silence. Their 'wailing' is accompanied by the metallic rumble of trucks and the crunch of worn gearboxes. The Berbers cling to the back of the trucks and then spill out, still wailing as they near the racers' bivouac. They start at our end of the horseshoe. It is 5.30am and they begin tearing down the tents around us. One team collapses the poles and uproots the pegs, another drags off the hessian, bundles it and throws it on the back of the truck. 'They must be on bonus,' I think to myself as I scramble half-asleep from my sleeping bag. I throw my pack onto my sleeping mat and drag my worldly possessions a few yards from the tent as it collapses with a 'whumph!!!' and a cloud of hessian dust and sand. The squaddies already have their stoves lit and are back in their sleeping bags, bergens neatly stacked beside them. My gear is scattered halfway to Casablanca as I rummage around in the bottom of my pack for my Greenheat stove. There is something so simply, functionally beautiful about my little Greenheat stove. It consists of a tin can with a ring pull (resembling a large can of tuna and weighing in at a mere 250 gms). It has a detachable metal windshield clipped around the circumference which also serves as the pot stand. All I have to do is prise the top off the can, light the gel inside, pop on the pot stand and I'm cooking! It is brilliantly simple, brilliantly effective, a thing of beauty. I boil up some water and stir in some banana porridge and a generous helping of Complan. This will be topped up throughout the day with banana chips, power bars, glucose tablets and energy drinks.

A brisk breeze blows across the bivouac. I shiver as I finish packing my bergen, pin my race number to the back of it and to the front of the chest rig which carries my water bottles, the day's food, my compass and some anti-inflammatories. The night had been cold. My 750gramme sleeping bag wasn't really adequate.

I'm nervous, apprehensive about my fitness for the task ahead. It's all very real now. I calm myself by going over the morning's events. I had been covered in fine sand when I woke up. The wind had picked up overnight and there was sand everywhere. I had sand in my ears, in my hair, up my nose, in my sleeping bag and beyond. I had been putting off a major challenge since arriving at the bivouac: my first trip to the toilet. There had still been a toilet at that point and I had struck out towards it, grimly focussed on my objective. As I neared the plywood structure and the smell assaulted my nostrils my resolve had given way. I wasn't going any nearer without a full chemical/bacterial protection suit and breathing apparatus. I had resorted to plan B and found a spot in the desert, as secluded as possible given the six hundred racers and assorted officials and media in the immediate vicinity. I had crouched behind a rather sad, spindly little bush (more for the psychological comfort of it than anything else as it provided little or no privacy). 'No room for sensitive types out here' I had thought to myself as I squatted, pretending to be invisible as a media land-rover roared past presenting the awful prospect of my backside featuring on TransWorld sport.

I'm brought back to the moment by the movement of something tumbling by in the corner of my eye. It would seem that not all competitors had been as careful as me in dealing with their bodily functions. The breeze carries with it the unspeakable paper by-products of innumerable toilet trips. This incongruous human despoiling angers me. I had long had a nagging feeling that we humans had failed in our duty as stewards of creation. We had corrupted the earth in our attempts to dominate and exploit it. Global warming, extreme weather events, melting glaciers: we were tasting the consequences of what we had wrought.[15] While it might seem odd, even amusing, to connect climate change with discarded toilet paper, to me this despoiling, albeit small-scale, betrayed the same selfish, entitled attitude. Such waste is easily buried or placed in the containers provided, later to be burned in the incinerator which follows our bivouac across the desert. The organizers have repeatedly warned us about discarding water bottles (they even mark them with your race number and a discarded bottle carries a severe penalty). Why can't they do something about discarded toilet paper? Maybe they could ration that too and stamp it with our race numbers …

I stand in line to collect my water ration, still shivering in the desert morning. My ration card is punched with an old-fashioned railway guard's punch. Scientist Marty had come over from the media bivouac earlier to set up the heart-rate monitors and give us the radio pills. It's weird to think it's lodged there in my small intestine transmitting every sixty seconds

There is a palpable buzz in the air as the start approaches. Six hundred racers gravitate towards the scaffold. The flags of all the nations represented fly aloft over the start banner.

---

15 See Qur'an, Surat Al-Rum, 'The Romans', 30:4.

The banner reads '17th Marathon des Sables'. Huge orange inflatable 'sausages' carrying the MDS logo funnel the racers towards the start line. Patrick Bauer, the race director, clambers onto the roof of an MDS Land-Rover and delivers a rousing speech in French. He speaks of the majesty of the desert and the nobility and heroism of our endeavour. His assistant struggles with equal heroism to translate. Patrick counsels us to start slowly and to support one another. The speech builds more excitement and this ratchets up even further when dance music starts to pump out incongruously across the salt flat on which we stand and a helicopter does a spectacular low pass directly above our heads. It hovers noisily over us kicking up clouds of sand. A cameraman hangs out at a precarious angle filming the whole spectacle. It's a scene more glamorous than any I've yet participated in. It is 9am and 90 degrees Fahrenheit, and today I've got around twenty miles ahead of me across the Sahara. The butterflies, which have been gathering force in my stomach, seem to burst out through my heart as the tape falls and the race begins. Six hundred souls head off into the Sahara amidst a cloud of choking dust and pumping rave music, and not one of them is happier than me.

I waddle along towards the back of the (now strung out) pack. My gait is somewhere between a fast walk and a slow, shuffling jog. I probably look like some small, overburdened dung beetle, in sharp contrast with the gazelles, greyhounds and whippets who have now disappeared into the distance. I may not be graceful as I shuffle along with my bergen weighing in at almost a third of my 58 kg bodyweight, but my heart is filled with a magnificent elation. I feel big.

To begin with the ground was the flat, dusty, hard-packed earth of the dry lakebed. Then it turned to loose gravel with bigger, scattered rocks on uneven ground. Now I'm moving through small hillocks of sand punctuated by tussocks of dry, spiky grass. It reminds me of childhood trips to the seaside at Aberlady, just outside Edinburgh, except that we're hundreds of miles from the coast and it's 100 degrees Fahrenheit. The jebel which curves away to the horizon in the north looks biblical: dry red with crumbling shards ready to shear away from the rock face. Mick, Terry and I stay together. The soldiers and Ian are together, but moving faster than us. Joe and Dave set out together at a pace way beyond my capabilities.

Despite the absence of any kind of track I carry with me what the organizers call a 'roadbook'. This contains rules, information about the logistics of the race, detailed maps, compass bearings and detailed directions (including terrain and surface conditions). The roadbook says I should cross Oued Draa at the only dry point: but there is no dry point. Freak weather in the previous week has raised the water level. Still, there are huge, flat, slab-like boulders strewn close together across the oued so it's no problem to cross. The boulders are perfectly smooth, an indication of just how old they are. This oued only has water in it every seven years. How long has it taken to wash those rocks smooth? The feeling of exhilaration returns as I leap from slab to slab, unabashed as one of the many course photographers snaps away. I am grinning like a lunatic as I scramble up the far side of the oued and into an uneven, sandy stretch with the same desiccated shrub-grass. Beyond, about half a kilometre away, I see a ridge of dunes: the first.

According to the roadbook these are 'dunettes', but they look daunting enough to me. A burst of pace with the assistance of my trekking poles gets me to the top of the first small dune. Ahead of me I see ripple after parallel ripple of identi-

67

cal dunes, like waves on a hot, dusty ocean. They are beautiful. Beyond the dunes I see more biblical high ground. I look down at the footprints of the many who have already passed this way. I check the roadbook anyway. 'Aim for the pass in the hilly area, compass bearing 78 degrees.' I check the direction of the footprints against the bearing. Guess what? Everyone is going the right way. The dunes are quite small and they don't last long, but they're a taste of just how difficult this is going to be. I'm aware of some relief as I step out of the dunes onto hard-packed flat earth again and realize how hard I've been working in the dunes.

The strap of my heart-rate monitor is driving me crazy. It's sitting right on the soft tissue under my breastbone and it hurts like hell.

I'm heading for the pass in the low, rocky jebel ahead. There's a well-head to my right, a dry-stone circle with a rough, sun-bleached, weather-battered wooden cover. Astonishingly, beyond the well is a low, black tent, like Tent 58. Before the tent is a young Berber woman with a child on her hip. She is an imposing figure of dignity and nobility of soul in defiance of her poverty. How can anyone scratch a living from this place? It is beautiful, but there's nothing here. Absolutely nothing.

CP1 is ahead in the middle of the pass. Arriving there feels good and I pause briefly to soak up the atmosphere. The officials are smiling and supportive. I'm part of something great. Now it's 112 degrees by the compass all the way to CP2. I refill my water and I'm off.

It's been flat, stony gravel most of the way from CP1. I'm just starting the climb into CP2 between jebel Gara Masmouda and more crumbling hills to the south. I must be working quite hard as my heart-rate monitor is beeping and I don't know how to turn the damn thing off. It's still hurting badly, like a really severe stitch. The gang are all here at CP2; Jo and Gemma but no camera or sound (Tom and Mark). Scientist Marty's here too and has a go at sorting out my monitor.

Flat and sandy all the way now. Off to the North I can see the dramatic mass of jebel Aferdou Amgloul. It looks as if it's been dropped straight out of a John Ford movie or like the mountain in *Close Encounters*, but without the trees. I can picture John Wayne in *The Searchers*. What a movie.

The awesome, arid beauty of Aferdou Amgloul is becoming a test of soul and resolve. I've spent hours trudging across this salt flat. There are a billion black ammonites strewn everywhere, curled up, shell-like reminders of an age when all this was at the bottom of the ocean. Maybe I'm the first person ever to disturb this fossil. I'm tired now, the heart-rate monitor still hurts and my neck and shoulders ache under the weight of my bergen. Aferdou Amgloul just sits there taunting me, the only vertical breaking the endless horizontal, never appearing to increase in scale despite my best efforts to progress towards it. I'll need water soon, but a quick check in my roadbook suggests I've managed things well. Every time I think water, I drink water. I carry one bottle containing a litre of water and another with a litre of isotonic mix. I've cobbled together two pieces of plastic tubing like the stuff that's used for making homebrew. This means I don't have to take the bottles out of the chest-rig to take a drink. This seems to be working.

Despite appearances, there's not too far to go. I look up from the cluster of contours amid an otherwise featureless page in the roadbook. Mick had carried on when I stopped to check our progress and now he's a hundred metres ahead. I'm alone. It's absolutely still but for the breeze.

My God! I'm really here. I'm really here! I feel a joy welling up inside me. This is a joy I've rarely experienced and then always fleetingly. It's the joy of being right in the moment and knowing in my heart and soul that I'm absolutely where I'm meant to be, doing precisely what I'm meant to be doing. It feels like I've caught a glimpse of something sacred, just for a second out of the corner of my eye. It's something at once deep inside me and completely beyond. I've tried meditating, and every so often, once or twice, I've caught the shadow of something, something sitting there impassive, unaffected, still, and at peace. This *something* observes all my thoughts, my joy, my sadness, fears, angers, ideas and regrets as they stream past in a torrent. I get a sense that right at the centre, beyond the torrent and beyond the observer, there lies something more, something wild, something huge and unfathomable. The God of the Wild Places. I've just caught another glimpse. It's perfect. I'm free. My heart feels like it will burst, and I'm crying.

It's great to get into Tent 58. Everyone is in high spirits. We've all had a pretty good day. Things have gone well for me: I've made sound decisions. My feet are in good shape. I've prepared them well, training for months with no socks in order to toughen them up and rubbing surgical spirit into them over the past few weeks. I taped my toes and the balls of my feet this morning with a coating of tincture of benzoate underneath as an adherent to stop the tape coming off when my feet sweat. It worked on the Thames Meander and it seems to be working here. I had also opted for an Arab head-dress rather than my desert hat. Steve P from the Thames Meander showed me how to tie it Berber style. It works a treat, but the guys in the tent are giving me a hard time because my sweat has caused the head-dress colour to bleed and it has dyed my head Moroccan blue. The heat has also melted the glue on my sand gaiters so I'll have to do some repairs. The only real problems I've had today have been the weight of my pack and the heart-rate monitor. My pack was fine in training, but things are different out here.

Not everyone has been so fortunate. Mick has developed a nasty blister. Shona seems to be struggling a bit too. She doesn't look so good and the urine sample she provided for Marty is a worryingly deep yellow. I think she's quite dehydrated. I've also heard that one of the Americans has pulled out. His feet are really messed up. Apparently, he'd made some bad decisions regarding his choice of footwear. I took things slow and steady today. My goal is to complete this thing. I may try to pick up the pace later when my pack starts to lighten up.

I lie in my sleeping bag looking out at the stars through the open sides of the tent. I've never seen such a sky: deep, inky blue spattered with more stars than I could ever have imagined and brighter than I thought possible (there's no artificial light out here to diffuse their impact). I think back to my moment at Aferdou Amgloul and my heart sighs with delight. I don't want to get so caught up in the task of getting to the next CP that I miss out on the wonder of this place. I want to keep my eyes and my heart open.

I am woken many times in the night by the ever-strengthening winds which carry the omnipresent sand and drive it into every crease, every article of clothing, every item of food. There is no escape from it.

Stage 2: Monday 8th April. Oued Mird - S/E Bounou. 36 km.
I woke up shivering at about 4am this morning. It's amazing how cold it gets in the early hours. The Berber onslaught at

5AM was only marginally less of a shock to the system today. The wind was wild throughout the night, burying everything in a layer of sand and tearing at the tent. None of us got much sleep.

I eat a breakfast of banana porridge, Complan and sand, which grinds and crunches between my teeth. I tape my feet and begin to pack my bergen, a little more efficiently now after some tuition from the British Army contingent. Big Mick stands in line for our water, a clutch of ration cards in his hand. All the while the sand-laden wind works its way into eyes, nostrils, ears, shoes and clothes. It clings to the P20 sun block. This is very effective stuff supplied free to competitors, but the combination of P20, wind and sand has left my skin the texture of glass paper.

It's getting close to 9am now. All my chores are done and the hanging around is nearly over. Patrick is back atop his Land-Rover. His assistant relays warnings that today will be a lot tougher than yesterday. The wind snatches at his legionnaire hat and whips the legs of his desert issue combat trousers as he stands over us. Above him the flags of the start line flap violently in the wind. The tape falls and we run into the swirling sand.

This is tough going. We've dropped into this riverbed at Oued Mird after following the edge of some crumbling sandstone hills across ankle-twisting loose rocks. I'll be amazed if everybody gets through that section without any serious injuries. This sort of terrain demands caution and we're moving slower than yesterday. Now, here in the oued, the going is really nasty. It's horrible stuff to try to run on: soft, gluey sand. There's a sort of dry crust on top with fine, clinging sand beneath which sticks to your shoes. It's like trying to run on day-old rice pudding and we've slowed to a walk again. It's very energy-sapping and my calf muscles are tight and aching already. My roadbook says we climb out of the oued soon, but then we're straight into a 5 km sandy stretch before a climb up to CP1 which is at the top of a pass. (That seems to be the nature of checkpoints.) It's hotter today and this damned wind has been blowing straight into my face all the way. It's exhausting to push against it.

CP1 looks like the moon: barren, desolate, pock-marked. There is a low hillock to the South as we leave. It provides a little shelter from the curse of wind-blown sand, but not for long. Now we start into a section of dunes: Erg Tomnarch. We thread our way through, and sometimes over, the small, mathematically-regular dunes and the scrubby tamarisk trees. Mick is having bad foot problems and this is starting to slow him. He looks worried and the jokes have stopped.

The wind has been ferocious since we left the dunes. For a while we were in amongst an area of vegetation and more of the scrubby tamarisk. This took the power out of the wind for a couple of K but now, out here on the flat, open sand, it's hellish. Any area of exposed skin is whipped by stinging grains of high-velocity sand, and it's still blowing straight at us, no matter what compass bearing the roadbook indicates. We try draughting. A small international team of us have been blown together and each of us takes a turn at the front to absorb the worst of the wind for a while before peeling off and falling in at the back of the line. The next man in line takes over for as long as he can stand it. And so on. It doesn't really work. We've all slowed to a slogging walk, struggling in the face of the storm. Visibility is down to a few metres. More low dunes loom out of the murk. It will almost be a relief to get in amongst them. At least they might provide some respite from this damned wind.

The sight from the top of the first dune through the sand haze is spectacular. Dune after dune, twisting and mingling like the folds in a brain, all seen as if through a sandy veil. This is going to be tough. There's no way around these. No way to thread a path through. They're arranged in contorted rows, wave after wave. The only way is up and over. My thighs burn and my heart pounds against my ribcage. I'm struggling. For the first time, I'm afraid. I'm not like these people. How long can I keep this up?

I make it through the dunes to CP2. Scientist Marty tells me that everyone is struggling today and we're going well, somewhere in the middle of the pack. But I just keep going. I make it through the final set of dunes in this stage. I make it across the last couple of kms of ankle-turning, stony flats. I make it to bivouac 3.

I sit at the open side of Tent 58 chewing biltong and waiting for my stove to boil, observing the thoughts as they run through my mind like tickertape. I struggled today. The terrain was tough, even before the dunes. The 'rice pudding' section really took it out of me. The two sets of dunes took a further lump out of my energy reserves. I had thought I was pretty fit in the run up to this, after a year of hard training, but the past few days have been a serious work-out. My muscles are taut and hard after only two days. The tiny amount of fat I did have on me has gone already. I was very glad of the checkpoints today, especially the second. It was a great relief to sit with the weight of my pack supported by a small dune. The pack is tough on my shoulders and neck and it's giving me a permanent headache. That second set of dunes was hard work. I was really low in there, emotionally and physically.

It was strange though. Every time I ate a handful of banana chips it made a difference. A few minutes later I would perk up and the emotional fog would lift. The final stony stretch seemed to go on and on. In the distance I could see a faint line of competitors snaking off through the haze. I was elated when I got in. Then came loads of faffing around with the TV stuff: weighing-in, urine samples, heart rate monitor, etc. I kept forgetting bits and pieces: first the monitor, then the urine sample and ended up doing about another km between Tent 58 and the control tent. I wasn't so happy after all that.

It's a shame really. The beauty of the second lot of dunes had been lost on me. I had just wanted to get in. The welcome had been great when I did get in. Lots of slaps on the back and congratulations. This felt good. Mick had to go to Doc Trotter's about his feet. Things don't look good. They did a real job on him and he's in agony. They had to cut fairly deep to avoid the danger of infection.

I'm really tired. Dog-tired. The backs of my legs are badly burnt. I don't know if you can put P20 on burnt skin. I guess I'll find out tomorrow. God I'm tired.

Stage 3: Tuesday 9th April. S/E Bounon - Oued N'am.

The atmosphere is subdued in Tent 58 this morning. Big Mick has pulled out. His feet are destroyed, and he can hardly stand. We've all been giving him a fairly wide berth, and he's gutted. Two years and around £2500 spent. All this to be put out with lousy blisters after two days. I saw his feet last night when he hobbled back from Doc Trotter's. They're bad: blister under blister, big and deep. He's sitting a few yards away with his head in his hands. Gemma and Jo from Granada TV are trying to console him. He's probably best left alone. I don't think he wants to do a piece to camera right now. For all his tough exterior and Parachute Regiment background, he's heartbroken.

There's something very powerful about men's tears. As I watch him sitting in the sand with his head in his hands, I'm reminded of the tiny, ancient, carved basalt figures of the 'Grieving Man'. They've been found all over Europe. There is something profound about the very masculine grief represented by these figures. This place and this experience have punched a hole in all the protective male armour, straight through to that same lake of grief I'd thought about when I was crossing the ice in sub-arctic Finland a couple of years ago. For him this is about more than a race, I think. I guess that's probably true for most of us. We've all got our reasons for being here. God, it must be heart-breaking. I don't know what to say to him. 'Leave him be' is what the soldiers advise. They seem to know about these things.

3 km of stony flats, then straight into more dunes. These are the same low, brain-like dunes, but with stunted tamarisk and the occasional stretch of open, flat ground. I seem to be coping better in the dunes today. It's amazing what the human body will tolerate and even adapt to.

The wind is bad again. It seems to still for a while around dawn but then gradually builds through the morning until it's raging in the afternoon. There's a palm grove to the north just now, providing a little shelter for the moment, but it's still blowing pretty much straight at us. It's soul-destroying, this constant battle against the wind. It's beginning to feel personal, as though the desert doesn't want us here.

I'm going quite well, and managing to stay with Terry. I'm pleased about that. He's strong but I'm staying with him so far.

It's hot today, the hottest yet. I'm glad to get to CP1: my water is gone. Collect water, fill bottles, mix in isotonic and move on. It's straight into more dunes, although there's a bit of a track through these. According to the roadbook and this morning's briefing from Patrick, we pass through a casbah today. That would account for the track.

We reach a stretch of open ground. Ahead I see some kids harassing a group of German racers. The same polyester sweaters, tatty trousers and smiley faces. We're next on the hit list. The hands are outstretched. They don't want money. They want 'scrivo' pens, pencils, anything to write with. They're hungry for learning. 'Bonjour madame!' A scruffy, tousled 8-year-old is beaming up at me. 'Bonjour madame, Scrivo?' Bonjour madame indeed! So much for my Ranulph Fiennes, tough guy, world explorer image. I look up and ahead. Sure enough, Terry heard him too. I can see his shoulders shaking up and down as he laughs. I can only put this case of gender confusion down to the fact that Terry is ahead of me and he's well over six feet, I'm not, and my four-day growth is covered up by my face buff. I laugh and drop a few coins into the outstretched hand. He scuttles off, no doubt in search of scrivo, past the women going about household tasks alongside their crumbling adobe dwellings. They watch us go by, some even wave, but all draw fine scarves across their faces with a graceful, dignified movement. There are kids everywhere.

We're crossing a wide, flat space. I think it's a dry riverbed. A quick glance at the roadbook confirms: Oued Moulih. There's a track and telegraph poles and more kids, teenagers. One of them is hassling an Italian racer. The Italian pushes the kid aside roughly. I'm nervous as I approach the group of teenagers. What will I do if they start hassling me? But they don't come near me. There's a slight climb up out of the oued. I'm crossing some sort of village square. There are children everywhere and women and, for the first time, men. They're all out to see the mad foreigners pass through their casbah. The roadbook says 'Mhamid El Rhozlane'. There are a couple of MDS Land-Rovers. Gemma and Jo are here, and Tom with his camera; no Mark though.

'Bonjour madame!' Another smiling eight-year-old, another shoulder-laugh from Terry. We pass through an adobe archway and enter the casbah. It's a maze of narrow alleys and intriguing doorways and tunnels. Women covered from head to toe stroll by with huge baskets on their heads. Overburdened donkeys struggle past, driven on by squinting men brandishing switches of thin, springy wood. Groups of men gather conspiratorially in doorways. I confess I'm reassured by the presence of the Moroccan policemen scattered here and there. I know this has nothing to do with the people of the casbah. It's all about my fear, projected on to them.

This is way off the tourist trail, all part of Patrick's plan for us to 'meet the people of the desert'. I'm sure they are a great people, but I struggle with people. I never know how to be. What I really want is to be back out in the desert.

There are still locals to-ing and fro-ing as we exit the casbah and start into some more palm groves and other scrubby cultivated land. The kids are still begging and it's still hot. It's not so windy here though: the wind must have dropped for the time being, or perhaps they built the casbah here for that reason. There's a lot of MDS activity. Several organization Land-Rovers have passed us with nonchalant Frenchmen giving thumbs-up signs out of open windows. I can see CP2 looming up ahead at the end of the palm grove. Tom, Sandy and Ian are there too.

Sandy is trying to sort out his feet. I can see from his face that it's not good. He was having trouble yesterday but today's heat has really messed him up.

A sandstorm is blowing up again. The CP officials advise us to stay in groups, so it's team 58 all the way through to B4.

We've passed through more dunes and a dry tributary of Oued Draa. Sandy is really suffering. The others counsel me not to slow my pace on account of him. He'll just get slower and slower if we adjust to his pace. They sound as if they're talking from experience. Who am I to question?

I never thought I'd ever find myself in the middle of the Sahara Desert talking to a soldier about God, but that's exactly what I've been doing for the last hour, as we make our way through the oued. There is just enough distance between us and the others for the conversation to be a trusting and private one. My prejudiced idea of the one-dimensional squaddie is fast evaporating.

We all come into Bivouac 4 together, past a Moroccan military check-point. The time has passed so much more quickly with company, which even seems to have made the going physically easier. But I don't think Sandy feels the same way. That was a phenomenal effort on his part. He's decided to risk Doc Trotter's. He wasn't so sure after he saw how they dealt with Mick's blisters. They don't mess about. First, they pierce the offending blister to release the fluid, then they cut away everything that's not good skin, right down to the raw skin. Finally, they douse everything in powerful, pink iodine. It's like a production line in there, or perhaps abattoir is more apt. I don't want to go there if I can avoid it at all. The screams of grown men are enough to put anyone off.

I've had a pretty good day today. I've felt stronger than I did yesterday even though the wind has been, if anything, worse at times. The wind in Tent 58, generated by Tent 58, can also be classed as a force of nature. I dread to consider the adverse impact we are having on global warming.

I've missed big Mick today. He's opted to stay with the bivouac for the time being rather than go back to the hotel, so he's ferried from bivouac to bivouac by truck. It was great when we got in today. Mick had tipped the Berber workers $5 to shore up our tent against the wind to stop it flapping around so much. They've shovelled sand around the base and added a couple of extra pegs. He'd also cleared the rocks from under the mats that make up the floor of the tent. He's chipped in with the little tasks that require so much effort when you are tired, like collecting the water and stacking it in the tent. He even made me a cup of tea when I got in. He's showing a lot of character, and he's making us laugh again.

I'm pleased I managed to keep up with big Terry. He covers ground at a good pace. I'm really getting the hang of the trekking poles. I've got the technique now and with no more effort than it would take to walk I'm moving at a slow jogging pace (which is still more like a walking pace for Terry, whose stride-length is about twice that of mine). We kept a good pace today. We passed loads of people who had set off running and had 'blown up' after a couple of hours. If I push too fast I know I won't make the distance. It's a balancing act between pace and time. I don't want to run out of steam. But if I go too slowly it means being out there for too long in the heat and that's equally debilitating and could lead to hydration problems.

My knees hurt tonight. In fact, everything hurts except the top of my head and my elbows, and now the combination of sun and wind has caused my lips to blister, another little misery on top of all the others. It's been a pretty good day though. I'm stiff, sore, wind-burnt, sun-burnt, filthy, smelly and stained red, brown and blue with sand, iodine and Berber dye, but I'm still in there.

Stage 4: Wednesday 10th April/Thursday 11th April. Oued N'am - Lac Iriqui. 71 km.

I've got the morning routine sorted now, although I'm still not as slick as the squaddies. I got my stove going in no time and breakfast's nearly ready. Food is just pure fuel now, regardless of what it is or what it tastes like. Today's breakfast is the usual porridge and Complan but I've also mixed in a sachet of freeze-dried spaghetti Bolognese. It's good. I'll need it. Today marks the start of the long stage. I've been worried about this since the day I signed up for this thing. 71 kms, almost two marathons back-to-back across brutal terrain. Apparently last year Patrick was criticized in some sections of the media for allowing 'The Toughest Footrace On Earth' to get too 'easy'. I think he must have taken it personally. Normally his race features what Patrick terms the 'dunes day' (even this is rich given that there have been dunes every day). This is followed by what they call the 'non-stop' stage (usually between 70 and 80 kms). This year, however, he's decided, in his wisdom, to put the dunes stage right in the middle of the non-stop stage. 28 kms of dunes smack in the middle of Stage 4: a 71 km epic. These are not going to be the kind of dunes we've experienced so far (although they threw some of those in for good measure at the start). No, this is the dreaded Erg Mhazil, some of the biggest dunes in North Africa, and that means some of the biggest in the world. They rise to literally hundreds of feet in places. Everybody is apprehensive, even the elite runners.

Not even the crazy racers who have done this race many times before have tackled Erg Mhazil in the middle of the non-stop stage. This is serious. Some would say insane.

There are two starts today. The top fifty racers are held back for a couple of hours while the rest of us plough on. I think the idea is to cut down on the advantage they get from arriving at the bivouac early and having loads of time to rest up. Also it stops the field getting so spread out as to be impossible to keep track of. That could be dangerous out here, fatal even. To be honest, I don't really care why there are two start times. I'm too busy worrying about getting through this stage in one piece. This is the one everybody is scared of. This was the main topic of chat on the website in the months running up to the race. This is the big one, the ultimate test.

Ian, Sandy, Terry and I are in amongst some low, rolling dunes when the Ahansal brothers pass us. First Mohammed, then Lahcen. They are an awesome sight. They look so fresh, even at this stage, as if they're out on a training run. Their running action is smooth, steady, efficient and ludicrously fast considering the terrain. Their metronomic pace hasn't altered since the start line on day one, and it's beautiful to watch. I'm tired already, and struggling in these dunes. An anxiety begins to bubble up inside me. These are molehills compared to the monstrous Erg Mhazil. Sandy is in bad shape, grimacing and looking down at his feet as he goes, but he's still with us. I don't know how much more of this he can take. This section of dunes will see us all the way to CP2.

We've arrived at CP2. Sandy has called it a day. I'm amazed he got this far. No fuss, no drama. He just told us he was out, wished us luck for the big dunes and walked away, dumping his bergen on the tailgate of the MDS Land-Rover as we got into the checkpoint.

It's like some kind of sick joke. We all know we've got to cross Erg Mhazil tonight. It's there in our thoughts all the time like some threatening spectre. The wind has been blowing in our faces all day, doubling the effort needed, and we've slowed again to a grinding walk. My left hip hurts badly. There's an ache deep inside the joint and the hip is clicking and grinding in its socket. And the dunes, the damned dunes. We're nowhere near Erg Mhazil but it's all bloody dunes. They sap the energy from my legs and drain my spirit a little more with every step. I check the roadbook. Even in my current predicament I manage a smile. This has to be the best roadbook entry yet; 'Exit small dunes and head West (compass point 275 degrees) towards small pass where there is a dromedary skeleton.' You don't get that on the London marathon! So here I am struggling along with my pack and my dodgy hip in a place that kills camels. It's absurd.

CP3 is just beyond 'dead camel pass' on a salt flat. Patrick has recommended resting up and gathering strength for a while at CP3 before starting into the erg. The checkpoint officials are preventing anyone from going in alone, insisting on small groups for safety reasons. Squaddies Tom and Barry are leaving CP3 as I arrive. I prise my pack off stiffly and stretch, watching them as they head for the massive obstacle in our path. They look so tiny and insignificant when framed by its yellow mass.

The sun begins its descent behind the high dunes of Erg Mhazil. I haul myself to my feet and re-shoulder my burden. My shoulders ache. I have a knot in the back of my neck where the seventh vertebra is. A discomforting thought has been knocking at the door of my consciousness for the past few hours. Sandy, a commando and veteran of the notoriously tough

P-Company selection, has been beaten by this mad race, the skin on his feet macerated and separating from the flesh. How is it possible that I'm still here? Me, the 58-kilogram school-teacher? It's as if logic has been suspended. The past three days have been amongst the toughest of my life. The thought of a further 100kms in even tougher terrain is horrifying to contemplate. I feel nauseous and my head is pounding. Every square inch of my body is screaming at me to stop, as now, at the mid-point of this brutal stage, I begin the ascent into Erg Mhazil. I look upwards at a mountain of golden-yellow sand, a silver line shimmering at its elegant crest as the sun goes down. The sky darkens revealing myriad desert stars. The wind is light now, blurring the perfect crests of these *Lawrence of Arabia* dunes. I smile ironically as I think of a North London training run when I almost ran into Peter O'Toole as he stepped out of his garden gate. I had to sidestep dramatically to avoid him. It is still just light enough to make out the tracks of previous runners snaking upwards ahead of us.

This is nasty. My legs are burning, my heart pounding already. The damned heart-rate monitor is going nuts again. I press all the buttons randomly until it stops. That's going to piss Scientist Marty off when he tries to analyse the data. An irrational surge of anger shoots through me aimed at Marty and his measurements. This just isn't about the numbers. Doesn't he get that? This is about so much more. But I'm in pain and I'm looking for someone to blame. This heart-rate monitor has been hurting me since day one, no matter how I adjust it. I want to throw it into the desert, but I don't.

It's too dark now to see enough to plan a route through the dunes. The wind is getting stronger all the time, driving painfully into my eyes and stinging my skin. Ian, Terry and I are working from a compass. In his address to the 'great unwashed' this morning Patrick had made much of a new innovation, a laser situated at the far end of the erg which would shine up into the desert sky and guide us weary travellers safely through the dunes. In reality we can't see ten feet in front of us because of the wind-blown sand. It forces my gaze downwards in a futile attempt to defend my eyes. Over the last few days my sunglasses have protected them from the worst of sand and wind but now, for the first time we're moving in the dark so I can't see a thing if I wear them. The wind drives sharp, stinging grains deep into my eyes and creates a choking dryness in the back of my throat. I put my sunglasses back on and stumble forward blind. I can see neither Ian nor Terry. I take the glasses off again and catch a glimpse of Ian's orange pack ahead through the murk. We struggle forward, the blind leading the blind.

Hours have passed. Miserable hours of agonizing, frightening purgatory. We are in the middle of a full-blown monster of a sandstorm. It's hellish. We can't see to negotiate a route through the dunes and are forced to follow a bearing, scrambling up and over each dune. I launch myself at yet another sand mountain. My thighs burn as if some awful, corrosive chemical is being pumped into them. Step after agonizing step, I battle upwards. I sink up to my knees with each step, labouring to drag my legs free from the sucking sand and inching slowly upwards. Sand pours over the tops of my gaiters and into my shoes. There's a childlike sobbing in my chest as I force myself on. I'm two metres from the top. The sand gives way in yet another spirit-crushing slide. I begin to slip backwards. Scrambling and struggling desperately on all fours I somehow reach the crest. As my head clears the top of the dune, I'm hit full in the face by a sand-laden gale force wind. My eyes slam tight shut in a reflexive reaction to the searing pain. I slump there, spent. I gingerly prize open my eyes to see another identical dune straight ahead. It's unbearable. Will it ever end? Around me a group of twelve or so racers of all nationalities are dragging themselves to the crest. To my left a tall American is hauling his tiny Japanese partner to the top of the dune, screaming at her to keep going. She's sobbing her heart out, hanging from his hand like a rag doll. To my right a Spaniard is vomiting in the sand. The whole scene is grotesque, like a Hieronymus Bosch painting. We slide or fall to the foot of the dune and start the whole desperate battle all over again.

I can't do this. I'm not strong enough. It's not possible. They must call a halt to this.

But even if they did want to call a halt for safety reasons, there would be nothing they could do. They can't get a Land-Rover in here and the helicopter can't fly in this. The storm would obscure any safety flare if we did send one up. I want to stop here in the relative calm of this dip between dunes and crawl into my sleeping bag, but I've got to stay with the group. I've got to make it to the checkpoint. There is no alternative.

I don't know how many hours have passed, but it has been the most extreme, exhausting, hellish battle to get to this checkpoint. CP4 is midway through the Erg. They dropped the water and the officials in yesterday by helicopter. I was overjoyed and felt like crying when I saw the faint glow from its lights seeping over the crest of a dune. I thought it would never come. God knows how, but Terry is going to press on. I've got to sleep. I'm dead on my feet. Ian and I are going to kip here for an hour or two. There are bodies everywhere. It looks like a mini refugee camp. In the centre is one big hessian tent full of racers mummified in sleeping bags. There is no space inside and the mummies have spilled out onto the sand, half-buried by the windblown grains and looking like some Egyptian archaeological dig. Ian and I grab a patch outside the tent. I throw off my shoes and crawl blissfully into my bag. Something sharp stabs into my back and I get out fast. The word 'scorpion' flashes into my consciousness, but no, thank God: it's some kind of thorny seed case. The wind has blown loads of the things into my bag. I clear out as many as I can and crawl gratefully back in. It's beautifully calm in my cocoon. I tear open a packet of my beloved biltong, South African dried, spiced beef, and listen to the storm raging in the world outside. It starts to rain. What next? I'm too tired to care and crash into a deep sleep, in my cocoon, in the rain.

'You ready to go mate?' It's Ian's voice. It takes a few seconds before I remember the terrible reality of where I am and what still lies ahead of me. We're up and off in less than two minutes. The wind has dropped a little but the going underfoot is no easier. More heartbreaking walls of sand. More thigh-torturing, calf-knotting struggles over interminable dunes. I spit and curse and rage my way to the top of another one and collapse, spent, before gravity takes me to the bottom on the far side.

I pass Ian another liquorice all-sort and pop the last one into my mouth as we sit at the base of yet another accursed dune. What a night. The occasional stretch of flat ground is a much welcome blessing and a relief. But it never lasts long. The wind has dropped even more now and we can see the laser ahead. It's reassuring: at least we know we're heading the right way. I had been convinced we had missed CP4 earlier, when we were struggling desperately in the heart of the storm, trying to follow a compass bearing in dunes that all looked alike. The laser never seems to get any nearer though. We talk and trudge and talk and scramble up dunes and rest. Then we trudge on again. We try to find easier ways through but it's useless. The world beyond the double arc of our head-torches is a mystery. We begin to follow what we think is a way between two big dunes only to find our road barred by another wall of sand.

I hear an engine. It doesn't sound like a Land-Rover. Definitely not. Too small. More like a motor-bike. Two beams of light pierce the darkness, pointing skyward. A quad bike breaks the perfect curve of the dune directly ahead, tyres deflated to negotiate the steep slopes. 'Everything is OK, yes?' I have rarely felt less 'OK' in my life but answer in the affirmative. 'Yeah. How far to the checkpoint?' 'Not far'. 'How far?' 'Not far'. How very bloody French I think to myself as he turns and heads back the way he came. I figure he'll take the easiest route through. He won't get over the big ones in that thing. We try to follow his tracks but lose them after 10 minutes or so and soon we're back in the torturous routine.

I see it! Through a dip in the dunes ahead. The source of the laser: CP5. We shout and laugh, shake hands and grab each other's shoulders. We've made it across Erg Mhazil.

Our celebrations are premature. I reach the top of the dune first. I expect to see the lights of the checkpoint, but it's like being in the mountains: the next ridge always looks like the summit, then, when you reach it, there's another, and another. Ahead of me are three, maybe four dunes. Big ones. We're not there yet, but the mere sight of the laser mast, the Land-Rover and the shabby tent feels like a victory.

Again the tent is full of sleeping racers. We throw off our packs, drag out our sleeping bags and crawl inside, exhausted, for an hour's sleep.

I awake shivering at around 6AM. I pull on my paper suit, the kind worn by prisoners when they're first arrested and their clothes have been taken away. It's the lightest solution for the morning chill of the desert. The building breeze feels ominous after the horrors of the night. The tent is empty now, deserted at dawn. My eyes are red and swollen, my legs leaden. We pack up swiftly, ready for the last push to the bivouac. A Land-Rover pulls up and the Granada crew spill out. They've been looking for me for hours. They give us the news: Ronnie got in, shattered and delirious, late last night. Alan came in during the early hours of the morning. Shona had struggled her way two miles from the start line yesterday before collapsing and being pulled out by the medics. She's pretty sick with some kind of viral infection. The camera rolls and I try to describe the horrors of the night. My words sound feeble as they leave my mouth, so inadequate an expression of such a miserable experience. I begin to sense Ian's impatience to hit the trail. I make my excuses. I'm still cold and opt to keep the paper suit on for now. The wind is gathering force as we head out into the 12 kms of salt flats between us and Bivouac 5.

This is a desolate, featureless place. Our progress across the saltpan of Lac Iriqui has become a battle against a vicious, sand-blasting gale. As ever, it's blowing straight in our faces. Each step forward is a miserable triumph, painfully, heart-breakingly slow. My mind has switched off. This has become a mindless, automatic slog, without meaning. The only purpose: to take the next step.

'This is impossible. I've got to rest. I think we should sit out the storm. We can shelter behind our packs.'

Ian looks at me incredulously.

'You can rest all you like when you get to the bivouac. We

don't know when, or if, this is going to stop. It could blow like this for days out here.'

He's right. I drag myself to my feet. The furious wind knocks me over before I can brace myself against it. The trials of last night and the crossing of this salt flat have left me in no doubt: the desert does not want us here. Our presence is an irritant, like flies on the perfect skin of some Bedouin princess. We had ignored her warnings in the preceding days and now the Sahara is making her outrage known. She intends to swat us.

I sink into a deep depression. All the while the storm blows. The desert is trying to push me back into Erg Mhazil. I fix my gaze on the back of Ian's heels. I just keep going. One small, forced step after another. I'm at my lowest point yet.

Then it looms in the distance. The grail. The banner. Bivouac 5. We jump up and down like lunatics in our joy at this beautiful sight. But the flat, featureless landscape is deceptive. Bivouac 5 is still a long way off, but we can see it. This makes all the difference. A tangible, visible goal. The end of the torture is literally in sight. Under normal circumstances the distance from CP5 to Bivouac 5 would have taken less than an hour. It has taken us five.

I pass through the narrow marshal's gate under the banner, totally depleted, disorientated and tearful. I'm confused, I can't calculate how many 1½ litre bottles make up my 4½ litre ration. The TV people are there. The last thing on my mind is Scientist Marty and the weigh-in and the rest. I stagger to Tent 58, where Mick and Sandy take over. They drag off my pack, roll out my sleeping mat and bag and manhandle me into the tent. Sandy stands over me with a 1½ litre mix of dioralyte (re-hydrating mix) and water. He watches me like a hawk until I've drunk the lot. Mick gets my stove going and cooks up a freeze-dried chicken curry (and sand).

The storm still rages. Fine sand is sieved through the mesh of hessian and hangs in the air like a mist. Scientist Marty has turned up and is trying to sort my eyes out. He cuts a Sidi Harazem bottle in half, holds the lid-end over my eye and pours the water in. It stings and makes little difference. I'm grateful for his concern. I still can't open my eyes. Every time I try to prise the lids apart a sharp, white pain flashes deep into my skull. The food and rehydration mix are doing their work. I feel the beginnings of recovery in my body. I am able to get to my feet. I hobble towards Doc Trotters. My feet are still OK, but my eyes are not. Everyone I pass *en route* moves with the same hobbling gait, the MDS shuffle. I feel my way to the medical tent like some subterranean creature exposed to daylight for the first time.

The young French medic performs the procedure with practiced efficiency. He's done it often enough over the past few hours. My head is tilted back, a tube is connected to a sealed, transparent plastic bag (like the blood or plasma bags you see in hospital dramas), which is secured high on a tent-pole. The doctor twists the valve open and my eye is flooded with a cleansing solution. It's an unpleasant, sickly sensation, but not unduly painful. I muddle my way through the weigh-in procedure and drop my heart-rate monitor off for Marty. He tells me I'm losing 2 to 3 kgs a day and putting most of it back on in the evenings. Apparently, this is a good thing. I don't really care. I'm too tired for this.

I stumble back to Tent 58. I've forgotten the urine sample

bottle. Back to the control tent. Back to Tent 58. Do urine sample. I don't know if Steve's expecting me to take this back, but it's not going to happen. I'm shattered. Ian is cooking some food. I thank him for getting me across the salt flats. He smiles ironically and thanks me for getting him through the second part of the dunes.

I wake up many times during the day and the following night with my mouth bone dry and my tongue sticking to the roof of my mouth. The wind is still in a fury. I think the last two days must count among the toughest of my life. I've had times before when I've been emotionally tested, at times almost to breaking point, but never has it been accompanied by such physical extremes.

My spirit was tested. I got through it. It was profoundly un-pleasant. I make a mental note never to do anything remotely like it again. Ever.

Stage 5: Lac Iriqui - Nord jebel Amsailikh. 42 kms.
The mood is very upbeat this morning. The wind has dropped and 70s disco classics are pumping from the PA mounted on top of an MDS Land-Rover. Donna Summer blasts incongruously across the desert.

It's odd. Only a few days ago, the prospect of a full marathon in desert conditions would have been terrifying. Everything has changed since Erg Mhazil. Nobody seems daunted by to-day's stage. We've come through the Big One, literally 'through the storm,' and we're ready for today's challenge.

The wind will pick up through the morning, I'm resigned to that; it doesn't worry me anymore. *I can do this. I know I can do this.* Physically, I'm in far better shape than I have any right to be. The human body is an extraordinary bit of kit. Water, pure, clean water, seems to have amazing restorative powers. I've been getting through nine litres a day. I make a note to drink more water when I return to my mundane existence.

I'm moving well, covering ground at a good pace across ammonite-strewn salt flats. The ground is rough and stony, tough on the feet and ankles. The views are spectacular: a huge 'John Ford' mesa (El Mdaouer Srhir) off to the South, a beautiful, biblical wadi, a dusty, red, crumbling canyon leading to a lush, green oasis of palms. It's classic desert.

I'm enjoying myself. I'm going well. Checkpoints are coming up faster than I expect (it's all relative after the long stage). Ian and I talk as we go. Our shared experience in the dunes and on the salt flats of the long stage has forged a bond between us. We relate on a level of trust far deeper than could reasonably be expected of two people who only met a few days ago. Steve P from the Thames Meander draws up alongside us. His progress is quick and efficient, polished by several MDS trips and one trip to Jordan for the Desert Cup. His pace is faster than mine. Foolishly I up my pace. Ian copes quite readily with the marginal increase in pace. But after a couple of miles my right Achilles tendon 'twangs'. I'm in pain and afraid. *Not now. Not at this stage in the game.* I recall the agony of the first time this injury occurred in my youth, in a karate class. If it goes the way it did then, I have no chance of making it. I curse my foolishness. I had vowed not to be drawn into trying to keep pace with anyone. I nurse my Achilles the couple of miles to the bivouac. Thank God it didn't happen earlier.

This is a peach of a bivouac site. A slight depression surrounded by small trees, startlingly green after all the dry reds, ochres and browns. I stand in line for my can of Coke (a reward from the organisation for making it this far). I sip my

Coke and chew on biltong in Tent 58. I'm so glad I brought the biltong. Its savoury spiciness is perfect after all the sweet isotonic drinks and energy bars. This is my last one so I'm really going to savour it.

Everything is very relaxed. Even the desert has given up her vendetta. The air is calm and still. Cooking is almost a pleasure in these conditions, and my sand-free vegetable curry is a delight. This will be my last night in Tent 58. Living in the wretched conditions of continuous sandstorms for the past week has left me with no great attachment to our tent. I have no romantic illusions about it. I'll be glad to get into a bath and sleep in a bed. But the desert has been good to us today. I reckon I'll finish this thing. In sha' Allah.

Stage 6: Nord jebel Amsailikh - Foum Zguit. 20 kms.

Things are very leisurely this morning with none of the mad urgency of previous mornings. The Berber workers are in no great hurry to get the shelters down: there's nowhere to move them on to today. I wish I still had some savoury food. I'm sickened by an excess of sweet, sugary, high-calorie stuff. It's 7am but I'm craving curry or spaghetti Bolognese. I force down some sweet banana porridge bulked up with Complan. I need to fuel my body, that's what's kept me going. My mouth and nose are in bad condition, burnt by the sun and scoured by the wind-whipped sand of the past week.

Right now there is an eerie stillness in the air. The bivouac is calm and quiet. Jo from the TV crew shows me a glimpse of myself in a make-up mirror. I look like Robinson Crusoe. The skin of my face is caked with the red sand of the desert. It reminds me of the red mud smeared on the faces of thirteen-year-old Maasai boys after they've killed their lion. This has been an 'ordeal'. It feels like an initiation. Something in me has changed because of the ordeal, and I feel connected to everyone who's shared this experience. The smell emanating from my once-pristine, now exhausted eco-mesh shirt is beyond repulsive. Never before in my life have I smelled so bad as to offend myself. I smell like I've recently applied a liberal spraying of 'Parfum de King's Cross Underpass'. It is truly revolting. The shirt, as well as smelling unspeakable, looks like someone has washed their car with it. Large, inexplicably tea-coloured stains merge with salty white tide-marks of dried sweat, and spread in concentric circles in all directions. I am a mess. I had loved my eco-mesh shirt when I bought it. It looked just right for the job: ultra-lightweight, loose-fitting, cool (in every sense of the word) and, crucially, sand-coloured. It had really looked the part. Now, in its exhausted state, I love it even more. It has proved itself up to the challenge and so, in my exhausted state, have I.

The start is approaching and a party atmosphere is developing, complete with the 70s disco music and even some stiff, hobble dancing. Twelve miles and this thing is over.

I feel very emotional as Patrick does his final speech. His words, the music, the atmosphere: but it's more than that. I'm twelve miles away from completing the Marathon des Sables. I'm really here. Me, Paul Pringle, twelve miles away from completing one of the toughest races in the world. I'm glad of my sunglasses and my Berber headscarf. Not because of the sand, but because they hide the tears rolling down my cheeks and the spidery channels they cut through the grime.

Even now I'm trying not to take anything for granted. Twelve miles is still a long way with my tendon in the shape it's in. It feels OK though. I did a lot of stretches last night and again this morning and that seems to have helped. It'll hold out. It would take a collision with an MDS Land-Rover to stop me now.

Ian and I walk five minutes, run five minutes. We're going really well, passing loads of people as we go, even the Para from the BOM website whose feet are destroyed (he's still way ahead of me in the overall rankings but passing him feels good anyway). After the final checkpoint of the race, we go for it, running all the way, flying past hobbling racers. I'm buzzing, exhilarated. I feel great. Where did this energy come from? We hit the rough tarmac of Foum Zguit, the village where the race will end. There are two kilometres to go and we're sprinting now. This is insane, but it feels good. The whole village is out, waving Moroccan flags and clapping as we go by. I see the finish line ahead and up my pace another notch in a good-natured race with Ian who has pulled away. There's a crowd of locals, racers and officials cheering us on. Ian is there at the finish line. He's stopped short of the line. He's waited for me. We cross the line together and he lights a cigar as I'm met by Patrick who hugs me and places a medal around my neck. My medal. My MDS medal. I punch the sky and snarl 'Yes!!!' Patrick laughs a delighted laugh. He knows what this means to me. His mission is accomplished. I am grabbed by the TV people. I can't connect with the emotion in the same way as I did at the start line. I feel fierce, not tearful.

An official thrusts a piece of local flat bread and an orange into my hand along with 1½ litres of life-giving water. I wolf down the bread, relish the juicy orange and set to work on the water. I sit in the shade of a large tent in the village square, savouring the moment, giving and receiving congratulations. Whilst waiting for the coach back to Ouarzazate I buy some gifts in a bazaar and exchange my battered shoes for a pair of the local leather slippers. The stall holder rips me off spectacularly, but with some style. Then I pay far more than the going rate for some local silver jewellery. At first I feel a bit small and naïve for having been ripped off. I soon let it go. I don't mind. I have enough, more than that man will ever have. I live in relative comfort as do my family. That man's family will eat well tonight. The generosity of others helped get me here.

I check the bag the merchant hands me before I hand over the money. I feel a stab of shame as he suggests that I don't trust him. 'Look, I don't count your money sir. I trust.' Maybe he's right. Maybe I'm a cynic. Maybe I'm just prudent.

Prudent, that's what I've been. I've managed my race well. Prudence got Ian and I to the end of this mad race. I ponder this on the bus journey. I ponder it in the luxury of a hot bath. I ponder it in the small courtyard of my hotel room. Soon I begin to question my prudence. A harsh, familiar, self-critical voice moves in to steal my gold. *I should have pushed faster from the start. I could have come in further up the field.* Could have, should have, could have, should have … I refuse to listen to that voice. I fight back. I managed my race well. My goal was to finish the race. I did that. If I'd done anything differently, maybe I wouldn't have made it. I did OK.

I settle into a quiet gratitude. Gratitude for the people I have met. Gratitude for the things I've seen. Gratitude for the desert. I collect my MDS 'Finisher' T-shirt. It's satisfying to know that I've earned it. I deserve this. I came through the ordeal. Something in me has changed and won't be the same again. I will return to my 'village' a different man from the man who stood at the start line a few days ago. The feeling now is one of completeness, the quiet joy of the Wild Places. No-one can take this from me.

I eat a wonderful meal of rich, sweet Moroccan stews with Tent 58. After the meal everyone heads for the bar. I watch them drink their beers and I feel sad and a little afraid as my awkwardness returns. I don't belong anymore; it's over. The mundane world is calling me back and I'm resisting that return. I buy a drink for Tent 58, make my excuses and go to bed.

I feel genuinely sad saying goodbye at Gatwick airport. My heart goes out particularly to Mick. His sadness seems to have been magnified by his return to home soil. Archie is there to meet me again. I'm grateful for this, and relieved. It would have been a struggle to get home by myself. There is a big, homemade banner on the door which says 'Welcome home Daddy'. I spend half an hour drinking tea, sitting with an awareness of just how fortunate I am. When she gets back from school, my little girl stands in front of me with a huge smile. There are big round tears in her eyes. She doesn't know what to do or how to react. She's had a tough week. In the playground at school one of the kids had said that people die in the desert. She's been frightened. I take her in my arms and give her a big hug and lots of kisses. She's changed so much in such a short time.

The Return

ON MY RETURN from Morocco I felt like I'd stepped off an aeroplane and onto a rollercoaster. I arrived home on a Monday afternoon and started a new job on Tuesday morning. Everything felt fresh and new: I was working in an attractive, bright building which contrasted starkly with the dark institutional oppressiveness of the one in which I'd spent the previous thirteen years. I was still working with children with learning difficulties but was no longer weighed down by the bureaucracy of the state system. My body still ached from my adventure, but I was full of optimism and energy. On that first morning my friend, and now colleague, Tony co-opted me into demonstrating star jumps and hops in the movement studio with a group of autistic children. My shattered limbs ached and complained with every movement, but I was happy. It was an unfamiliar feeling: I was at work, yet I was relaxed and content. The years spent 'treading water' were over. Something had shifted in my psyche with the whole MDS experience and this shift was now showing up in my life. This sea-change was no coincidence. This transformation was a direct result of connecting with purpose in my life.

In those first few months after my return it seemed that everyone I met wanted to know all about my adventure. My stories were met with gasps of amazement. My male friends in particular would shake my hand or slap my back in approval and admiration. I was nourished by this attention, along with my memories of the race for a number of contented months. I was happy in my new job and looked forward to the screening of the documentary.

Weeks and months went by and people's interest waned. I realised with a sinking feeling that there was a danger that my desert adventure could become 'the only significant thing I ever did.' I became restless and ill at ease again. Was that really it? Was it all over now? Was I destined to slip back into anonymous drudgery? That couldn't be what fate had in store for me. It just couldn't! When I had first enquired about the MDS I'd read in the literature about the depression which can strike some people when they get back from the desert. A number of the veterans had commented that almost everyone says 'Never again' at the finish line, but inevitably, a couple of years later, familiar names start to crop up on the entrants' website. I found myself back in the position of merely turning up for life, not really 'living'. This was made worse by the intensity of my desert adventure. I had that peculiar yearning sadness in my chest again. What was that feeling about? Why did it have such power over me? What was I longing for? I needed something of the clarity and purpose I'd felt after my 'rites of passage' experience in the New Forest. I needed to go deeper. I needed further initiation, a new Vision Quest.

'Warrior Monk.'[16] I'd liked the sound of that when I first heard about it, soon after my initial weekend rites-of-passage workshop some years previously. Warrior Monk was facilitated by Bill Kauth and Onzie Stevens and the purpose of their retreats was to offer a way of balancing Spirit and Soul in a person's life: the 'Big Picture' with the specifics, action and doing with mindfulness and being. I decided to sign up. All I will say about the workshop is that I got what I came for, and more. I emerged from this latest phase of my ongoing 'Initiation' with a new mission. 'I nourish souls by showing glimpses of the God of the Wild Places.' This felt so right. I loved the sound of it in my mouth. Four years or so previously, the first phase of my initiation into mature masculinity had helped to free me from the shackles of a small, stifling existence. My new mission was set to catapult me onwards into the adventure that my life had become. I'd rediscovered a wildness in my heart and soul and now I needed to power that wildness up in order truly to fulfil my mission. I knew I had to go out again and seek the God of the Wild Places myself, to be touched by that awesome power. I couldn't give it away until I could feel it deep in my own heart. Another signpost on the greater journey.

Shortly after the MDS I'd heard about a race in the Yukon Territory in the far northwest of Canada. The Yukon Arctic Ultra was billed as the world's toughest and coldest human-powered race. I had been immediately drawn to it but I was married at the time with a young child. I felt that my entering the race would be asking too much of my family. It was a potentially

16 warriormonk.org

dangerous event and I couldn't just keep disappearing off to various parts of the world to do mad things, could I? A year had passed since the Sahara multi-marathon and I had felt the Yukon race sitting in my guts for much of that year. Now I'd made a decision. I sat in a circle of 'initiated' men and asked their support and counsel. I called Shona from the MDS who now worked for the UK promoters of the Yukon race. Twenty minutes later I was registered for the Yukon Arctic Ultra. Now I had to get in shape.

I had done little or no training for almost a year, and I was expecting the worst. My mind went back to those awful, painful early days of preparation for the MDS. Much to my surprise and relief I felt quite strong from the outset. I seemed somehow to have retained a base level of fitness from my MDS preparations. I ran with a moderately-weighted pack from day one and built the weight up quickly so that after two or three weeks I was running with around ten kilos.

Jo from the Granada crew had contacted me about the broadcast date for the documentary. She had mentioned that she was contemplating entering the Snowdonia marathon. This event takes place on and around Mount Snowdon, the highest peak in England and Wales, and is one of the toughest standard marathons in Europe according to many of the experienced runners I had met in the desert. The date of the race was still a couple of months away. I knew Jo had decided not to enter in the end but I realised that a race like Snowdonia was exactly what I needed as a focus in my preparation for the Yukon. I logged on to the website and registered.

Having a clear and not-too-distant goal gave a much-needed injection of purpose to my training. I worked harder and got out more often. I wasn't doing the miles I had put in for the desert race but the ease with which I'd taken to running again after such a long break made me feel reasonably confident that I was on schedule.

I like Wales. Snowdonia is spectacular: mountainous, wild and rugged. The deep, lush greens of the mountainsides, interrupted by slate-grey, rocky outcrops, lend the region a mystical, other-worldly quality. It would have seemed perfectly reasonable if Merlin had emerged from the mist as my little car wound its way around twisty mountain switchback roads *en route* to Mount Snowdon and the infamous Marathon. My then wife and child were with me. We'd driven for hours, much of the journey in heavy rain. It's a trip which always takes twice as long as expected, and it was late afternoon by the time we reached Llanberis and our guesthouse.

Our host was a big, gregarious man from the Midlands. He had a ready smile, a loud voice and a complete disregard for what anyone thought of him. I took an instant liking to him. He was well used to catering for runners entered in the Snowdonia race but was intrigued, and a little mystified by the whole concept of ultra marathons and wanted to know more. As I told him about the desert race and the Yukon race, he shook his head with delighted incredulity. He had a broad grin on his face and a familiar sparkle in his eye. Men often respond at a very deep level when they hear of such audacious, unjustifiable, gloriously irrational endeavours. Over and over again I've seen that same sparkle, that same fire, come into men's eyes when conversation moves into the realm of adventure. Normal men, in normal jobs, with normal lives light up. Their eyes widen and their gestures become animated as they share their own adventures or aspirations to adventure. I've seen this happen to the extent that they unconsciously clutch imaginary steering wheels and let out involuntary engine noises as they risk sharing dreams of driving through the desert in the Paris–Dakar rally. It's a delightful thing to behold.

The following morning at breakfast I found myself assailed by a familiar self-doubt. I'd only shaken off a nasty chest cold a few days before and wondered if it was foolhardy to attempt this race while less than 100%. My natural anxiety about the task ahead was raised several more notches by the sight of Mr and Mrs Perfect Specimen (and son) at an adjacent table. It became apparent that it was Mr Perfect Specimen who would be racing, but finely-muscled arms and lithe, powerful legs suggested that Mrs Perfect Specimen could clearly have left me for dead at the start-line had she been racing too. I think I could probably have finished ahead of baby Perfect Specimen! I remember thinking: 'Why do I keep doing this to myself? I just don't belong with these people.' There was a mad wrestling match going on inside me as these thoughts clashed with a kind of over-confident pride which whispered: 'Listen, you finished the MDS, this'll be a breeze.' I ate a light breakfast as this battle raged on in the pit of my stomach. Back in the room I comforted myself with the now familiar routine of taping my toes and feet and drinking some isotonic mix to make sure I was fully hydrated before the start.

We left the hotel and followed the purposeful stream of lycra-clad whippets and gazelles as they made their way to the start line at Nant Peris a mile or so along the Llanberis pass. I'd sorted out the logistics of registration, collection of race numbers and so forth the previous evening and to my surprise I was beginning to enjoy the atmosphere as I walked with the crowd in the cold morning air. I'd been a bit worried about the weather: Wales is not renowned for its tropical climate, but it was a perfect morning; bright, clear and cold. I almost convinced myself that I did belong. I looked the part. I definitely had the thin, wiry physique of a distance runner. I'd be OK. I knew from experience that I could push my body to do what it was told. I'd done 50 miles in a day on two occasions now. I'd finished a desert ultra. How difficult could twenty-six miles in Snowdonia without a backpack be?

But my stomach was still churning as I dumped the bag containing the fleece and windproof I'd been wearing into the back of the transit van which would transport it to the finish line. My daughter hugged me and I made my way down under the start banner and joined the waiting runners. Not quite subconsciously I placed myself in a spot in the back third of the assembled crowd, not wanting to appear cocky or over-confident. I felt acutely self-conscious as I looked around. Everyone appeared to be at ease: stretching, chatting, laughing. They were all so used to this world. I stood awkwardly on my own, longing for the start horn to sound when I would be free to focus on the painful simplicity of the task at hand.

I don't have too long to wait. The flag drops and, with a ripple of cheers and applause from a crowd of spectators I'm not used to seeing, they release me into the wild! I am faintly embarrassed as I run past the clapping crowd. My daughter waves and smiles a slightly awkward smile, not quite sure how to respond to this unfamiliar scenario. Mrs Perfect Specimen sits nonchalantly on a dry-stone wall with her child and claps and encourages as we all stream past. I feel comfortable and set a steady slow-to-medium pace, just like my training pace, being careful not to get drawn into charging off too fast in the initial excitement. The first four or five miles follow the A408 along the Llanberis pass, rising steadily on a long snaking ascent of 800' in the first four miles to Pen-y-Pass. I feel strong on the climb and keep to my rock-solid pace and I'm passing many of the people who'd set off too fast. Snowdon, or Yr Wyddfa to give it its proper Welsh name, rises majestically to our right where it will remain for the duration of the race as we do a clockwise circuit of the mountain. The feeding stations seem ludicrously close together after the Marathon des Sables: every two miles or so. I'd noticed while looking at the route details last night that there are eleven feeding stations on this course. Over an equivalent distance in the desert race there would have been two. I still make sure I drink water and isotonic alternately and grab a mini Mars Bar at each station. You have to give your body something to work with. We reach the summit of the pass and the vista opens up to reveal a spectacular mountain landscape: a broad valley dropping dramatically to the right into a mysterious dark lake before rising to the mass of Yr Wyddfa. Straight ahead stand layer upon layer of mountain ridges growing paler and more dissipated as they stretch into the watery light of the distance.

The road starts to descend and my pace increases. I'm moving quite quickly as the route drops 900' in eight or nine miles and I'm starting to feel the jarring in my knees and feet. Out of nowhere a motorcycle appears on my left shoulder and the rider's visor flips up to reveal a grinning Tony D. It feels good that my friend and colleague has ridden up from London specifically to support me in this race. It gives me a real lift to see him. He rolls alongside at running speed for a couple of miles and makes lots of encouraging noises about how strong I am looking. Then he roars off.

I spot Tony's shiny blue-and-silver BMW parked up by the bridge in Beddgelert, and there he is, camera in hand and full of support and enthusiasm. It's amazing the effect such encouragement has. Even the claps and cheers of strangers scattered along the marathon route make a difference, but Tony's focussed and energetic backing really spurs me on into the sharp climb out of the village. The route rises another 400 feet in only a couple of miles before evening out to a long, gradual descent into the village of Waunfawr. This stretch seems to drag on for ever and I'm very glad to see Tony's face appearing out of hedgerows every so often offering chocolate bars and cans of energy drinks to keep me going.

I'm starting to suffer and my pace has dropped. My right foot hurts badly and the tendons in my groin—the ones responsible for lifting the knees—are as taut as bowstrings and scream out with each step. From Waunfawr the route turns sharp right and onto an old quarry road. This road is steep and rough, more a track than a road, and now, at around twenty-three miles, I've slowed to a virtual walking pace. My foot hurts badly now, and severe bruising and the steep slope are exacerbating the pains in my groin. Tony shuffles alongside for a while, willing me on. At the high point of the mountain pass he points back the way we have climbed. I turn and my gaze is met by a staggeringly beautiful scene. The mountains layer away into the distance on my left as far as I can see in the late autumn light. Wisps of pink cloud hang motionless in an otherwise perfectly pale blue sky. Before me, where I had expected to see more mountains, lies the Irish Sea. The early afternoon sunlight makes the sea appear like a mirror spattered with unpredictable pools of mercury. The reflected pink wisp-clouds dance between those shifting pools. I am stunned for a moment by the dramatic juxtaposition of mountains and sea. Then it's time to slog on.

There is no road here and Tony will have to retrace his route and go the long way back to meet me at the finish in Llanberis.

There are only a couple of miles to go but the path is steep and rough, dropping around 900' into the village. My knees are suffering too now and my foot and groin are worse than ever. I have woefully underestimated this race and I'm paying the price. 'How difficult can twenty-six miles in Snowdonia be without a back-pack?' Very bloody difficult, is the answer.

I am well down the finishing order and feel embarrassed as I turn off the hill path and into the village. It is cold and the crowds have thinned to virtually nil, but my family are still there on the corner of the main street as I limp around the bend and head for the finish line at a feeble jogging pace. Tony is there too when I cross the line and provides much back-slapping and hearty congratulations. I need all the support I can get. I feel no elation. I feel ashamed at the five hours plus it has taken me to finish. That may extrapolate to a reasonable pace for an ultra, but it's poor marathon running by any standard, even in the mountains.

I hobble back to the B&B with a space blanket around my shoulders. I can feel my right foot swelling in my shoe. I drag myself up the staircase to the room and remove the shoe. There is an angry looking yellow, red and purple bruise running the length of the outside of my foot. It hurts like hell and is getting worse rather than better since I've stopped. I hop along the corridor into the blissful womb of a hot bath.

So went the Snowdonia Marathon: a real wake-up call for the Yukon. I had just over three months to get myself in better shape. I was out of action for the first three weeks waiting for the swelling and bruising in my foot to settle down and the pain to subside enough for me to get back out on the roads. But Snowdonia had done its job. It had focussed my attention on the work to be done in the time remaining before the

Yukon. It had, however, done little for my confidence.

A few days after arriving back from Wales I had dreamt of an incident long ago: a message I had taken on board in childhood about who I was. I would have been about thirteen or fourteen years old, sitting upstairs on the school bus with my friend Keith (who is still a friend all these years later). There were a couple of younger kids at the back of the bus acting up, making smart-arsed comments and firing chewed-up paper pellets from pea shooters. Keith turned on them and with a few well-chosen words intimidated them enough that their antics stopped immediately. Stopped, that is, until Keith got off the bus two stops before me when the whole routine kicked off again with a vengeance. Despite my protestations and threats the tormenting continued. I got off the bus feeling powerless and humiliated. The message I took on board? 'Some people have personal power and authority, and people listen to them; but I'm not one of them.' I've had exactly the same feeling on the 'phone to insurance companies, banks, telephone companies, even in the past when dealing with bosses or colleagues. I can't stay in my power. I become an ineffectual, bullied child. Painful as it is to admit, I feel like crying when this happens. It's all so familiar. I all too readily default to this feeling of powerlessness, of being at the mercy of the big bad world and the big bad people in it. And if that's the way I'm thinking, that's the reality I'll create. When I am in the desert or the mountains I know and accept that they are a far greater power than me. I respect that power and try to be in harmony with it, a part of it even. It's wholesome. It's right. It's the antithesis of the powerlessness I can feel in the mundane world of day-to-day aggravations. I feel truly alive, vigorous, vital. I feel my true power. Not the power to conquer, but the power of connection to all that is, the purity of God's creation. It feels like the true 'I', that same true 'I' that I've always sought. My hunger for initiation and my seeking to fill the empty, powerless shell, are one and the same as this search for the 'I'. More and more I bring that feeling back with me from the Wild Places. More and more I can touch it wherever I am.

I awoke one morning in the weeks after the Snowdonia race aware of a free-floating anxiety. It took the few seconds between sleep and wakefulness to locate its source. It was the powerlessness again. Would the big, bad insurance company keep its word and reimburse my money (my car had been vandalized)? When I left the flat for work I noticed the beer cans discarded in our front garden, tossed nonchalantly from our neighbour's window. This was a regular occurrence. Each time it happened, it plunged me into another round of anger, fear and shame. Anger at this man's lack of any respect or consideration, fear at the thought of confronting him (and the potential repercussions), shame at my failure to confront him and my self-adjudged failure to secure a better home in a better area for my family. Each discarded beer can chipped another sliver of self-esteem from the already fragile edifice and added more fuel to the perpetual motion engine of self-criticism as it pumped out its toxic fumes. I remember brooding on this on the twenty-minute walk to work, my right foot still aching and grinding after the Snowdonia marathon. (Maybe I should get it X-rayed.) An irrational fear built as I walked through the carpark and neared the building.

I sat through a meeting. Having adopted the long-practiced alert but detached demeanour which permits my mind to wander unchallenged, my thoughts settled on the Snowdonia Marathon. I rotated my foot under the meeting room table just to feel it twinge with pain. The action reconnected me with the raw experience of the event: the way something 'went' in my foot at around fifteen miles, the way my hips ground in their sockets on the steep incline at twenty-one miles, and how my knees screamed for respite on the interminable downhill into Llanberis and the finish line. I felt myself weeping inside, longing to be back there in the mountains, yearning for the painful liberation of it all. I desperately needed to go for a run but knew that my foot wouldn't take it for another week at least.

Someone was still reading the minutes of the previous meeting. A massive, familiar geyser of anxiety burst to the surface like Old Faithful. 'I can't do this for another minute' (said the voice of the mountains, the desert and the forest), followed closely by 'I have no choice' (the voice of the rent, the bills and responsibility). And so the battle for my soul continued.

I ploughed on through the afternoon and took a break to make a cup of tea. In the kitchen, the caretaker struck up a conversation in a slightly conspiratorial tone. Arthur is in his seventies, long past the age where he should be taking it easy, collecting his pension. I like Arthur: he reminds me of men I was surrounded by as a child. He's worked all his life. He knows how things work and seems able to fix anything. He was in the Parachute Regiment as a young man and occasionally recounts the stories. He's a decent 'what you see is what you get' working-class man, and I respect him. He told me that he was leaving as his hours had been cut to an hour a day and it was not worth his while on the minimum wage he's getting. I didn't know what to say. It's uncomfortable when someone I judge to have earned the right to respect suffers such indignity. Curiously,

I had felt a similar feeling on the day I realized I was earning more than my father. It just didn't seem right (he also knows how to fix things). Arthur's situation added to my feelings of despondency. In a tribal society he would have been an elder, an old warrior. His life-experience and wisdom would be valued and honoured, his stories of warrior exploits welcomed. We think we're so sophisticated, so advanced, but sometimes I think we've learned nothing. Things of real value, like wisdom and experience, are scorned while we worship the worthless and transient, celebrity and fame. Again, I felt the longing for something better, clearer, truer. We have lost so much.

I became aware that I had a headache from breathing stale, indoor air. In my heart and soul I smelled pine forests, husky dogs, the freezing air of the far north, desert dry sand, woodsmoke, biltong, sweat, adventure, pain, freedom. Never in my most pain-wracked moment in desert, mountain or forest have I longed to be back in a classroom or a meeting room. Never. Injustice! Something resonates deep inside me when I hear of it or see it happening. I felt the same outrage resonating in my chest on our last day in Snowdonia. The marathon completed and hearty breakfast devoured we had packed up the car for the homeward journey. Before getting on the road proper we decided to stop at the Welsh slate museum in Llanberis. There I got more than I'd expected. The sorry tale of the rapacious greed of Victorian industrialists, their brutal exploitation of the Welsh slate workers and the desperate struggle for survival of the quarrymen and their families, again brought the impotent anger to the surface. I listened to the stories of men working in the filthiest, most dangerous of conditions for wages which kept them in sub-poverty conditions. The hair on my neck bristled as I heard of the tragic end to the ill-fated Penrhyn strike of 1896, the quarrymen forced back to work after an eleven-month lockout, their children starving, no concessions gained. Meanwhile the quarry owners and slate exporters grew richer and fatter. The British empire was built on the backs of people like the North Wales slate workers, which was slavery by another name.

The sacrifice and integrity of the quarrymen, men who never travelled beyond the valleys and mountains of North Wales, render their lives well-lived in my eyes. I salute them and honour their stance and that of their families. They taught me a powerful lesson about courage, integrity and real endurance.

When I die, I want my life to have been a life well-lived. Our short trip to the slate museum reminded me that this doesn't have to be about conquering Everest or reaching the South Pole. I almost didn't write this book because of the voice in my head which tells me: 'Nobody wants to hear about your puny adventures, when other people are conquering the Himalayas or cave diving in Venezuela. You can write a book, but not yet, not until you've done something really impressive ... then people might be interested.'

If I listen to that voice the time will never come when I'm ready to offer something to the world. It doesn't have to be the perfect adventure. It doesn't have to be the highest, longest, toughest or the most painful. I made a stand in my life. I dared to do things differently and I've learned and grown so much from my adventures, it seems right to share it ... in all its imperfection. That's what this whole thing is about; how I started listening to the Voice of longing.

CHAPTER 8

Yukon Hyperborea

I FIND IT very difficult to concentrate on the mundane when I've got a 'project' on. This becomes more pronounced as the event draws nearer. The Yukon Arctic Ultra was no exception. As the start date approached I became more and more preoccupied with the race, almost resenting being asked to do my job (didn't they know how important this was?). My attention became almost exclusively fixed on the event. What was the current temperature in Whitehorse, the starting point? Was my sleeping system going to pass the pre-race scrutiny? (I'd had to cut corners for financial reasons). Were the native-style Mukluks the right choice for my feet? How could I best customize the injection-moulded kid's sled I'd bought in order to carry 23 kg of kit?

The list of things to do went on. My work wasn't the only thing that suffered. In the midst of all this 'stuff' I hadn't really seen how this project was affecting my family. I knew that my then wife had her concerns about the whole thing, and I knew that my daughter was angry that I was going to miss her tenth birthday. I wasn't prepared for her reaction when they dropped me off at Paddington station on a damp February evening. I'd

worked right up to the last minute and had packed my kit into my now very heavy sled the previous evening (not counting several dozen packs and re-packs in the preceding weeks). I now stood in front of the automated ticket machine failing to secure a standard class single on the Heathrow Express. I was approached by a drunken city worker who'd bought the wrong ticket and wanted to sell it to me at a knockdown price. My suspicious nature counselled me not to go for it, but I checked the ticket over and gave him his £10 (I couldn't get the machine to work anyway). When we got to the platform my daughter's face began to crumple. It was only when confronted by the sight of her big, round, sad, frightened tears that I realised how much this was affecting her. I felt a terrible combination of sadness, guilt, protective love and helplessness. I kissed and held her, and dragged myself away, waving and smiling unconvincingly as I went.

I had already strained my elbow lifting the sled awkward-ly from the car, and I continued the assault on my physical wellbeing with the transfer from trolley to train. What was it the website had said? 'The world's toughest and coldest human-powered race.' I'd managed to sustain my first injury on Platform 7 at Paddington. I sat in the train smiling at the ludicrous nature of what I was about to attempt (remember, people like me don't do things like this). I didn't know at this stage that there would be a physical toll to pay on this trip.

The twenty-minute journey to Heathrow afforded me the opportunity to mull over the anxieties of the previous few days. These were not, at this stage, anxieties about the race, but familiar worries about flights, connections, being on time and, above all, people. I'm not always great with people and my stomach churned at the prospect of the social demands which awaited me. I always end up wandering around awkwardly, looking for something or someone familiar to anchor me.

Bad news awaited me at check-in. I wouldn't be able to check the offending, way too heavy, sled all the way to Whitehorse. I would have to pick it up in Toronto and lug it around all night until the connecting flight left the next day. This was all down to tightened security arrangements, a stark reminder that the world had changed on that morning in September back in the days when I was training for the Marathon des Sables.

I scoured the departure lounge for likely-looking YAU participants, my eye settling on a relaxed-looking individual lying back with his legs crossed on his bergen—blond, crew-cut, mid-thirties, powerful build, understated, functional outdoor gear with Swedish flags, all held in place with an air of self-sufficiency. I knew where he was headed and I felt that all too familiar 'Who the hell do I think I am?' feeling. I just wasn't like these people. Each time I'd picked up an e-mail from the event organiser in the run-up to the race I had been faintly embarrassed at being addressed as 'Dear athlete'. Let's face it, I was no athlete. I was, as a dear friend had suggested prior to the MDS, an 'inspired madman'. (The same friend had added 'crazy diamond' for this event.) Part of me still couldn't own what I was doing.

The Toronto flight was not good. After a few hours I found myself deeply envious of the little Bangladeshi woman beside me who slept almost all the way, interrupting her sleep only to eat a little and beam a disarmingly open smile before dropping off again. The sleep of the righteous perhaps, or just the sleep of someone who'd recently got off a connecting flight from Bangladesh. Two or three hours out from Toronto I was faced with a dilemma: should I tick the box marked 'meat products' on the customs declaration or not? I decided not to risk the wrath of Canadian customs and my honesty led to all my biltong and one of my ready meals being confiscated. This was a legacy of the 'mad cow' disease which had decimated dairy farms across the UK a few years previously. I was not happy, but it was their country after all, and so their rules applied. I was too tired to argue anyway. I met Col, a fellow YAU participant (I can't bring myself to use the term 'racer', the preferred terminology among people who do these events. 'Fellow racer' would imply that I thought of myself as a racer. I hoped merely to survive the race and reach the finish line). Col, I was to discover, despite an unassuming and self-deprecating manner, really was a racer.

The few hours sleep I managed to grab on a bench in Toronto airport (with my sled!) were remarkably refreshing and I felt almost human as Col introduced me to Peter, the 'Viking' I had spotted in the departure lounge the previous day. Peter was an experienced winter ultra-racer. He'd completed his national service in the Swedish military and was a veteran of races in Alaska and across Scandinavia. Although he was modest about his own abilities and encouraging in his comments, I defaulted to feeling like a 'wannabe', an inadequate impostor. His innocent question on seeing my Mukluks – native style winter moccasins – 'Are you going to race in those?' led to my feeling that I had a big orange hat on my head with the words 'I have no idea what I'm doing' emblazoned across it in large tartan letters.

The reality of what lay ahead was beginning to hit me. I had to admit that my motivation for doing this thing wasn't just about 'being all I can be' and inspiring others to really live their lives. There was also, I'm slightly ashamed to say, a fair amount of pride. I had wanted people to be impressed when I told them where I was going to be in February and what I was going to be doing. Now came the scary bit: I had to actually do it.

The flight to Vancouver found me sitting beside Bob, who was bound for the slopes of Whistler with some friends (a group of middle-aged adolescents who spent the flight cracking dirty jokes and flashing soft-porn magazines across the cabin). Another, mercifully shorter stop in Vancouver hooked us up with still more 'racers', including Clive, a gregarious Welshman with an infectious enthusiasm for adventure in general and for races of this kind in particular. He was an experienced winter racer with an impressive CV. We had swapped e-mail messages in the preceding weeks and he had been an invaluable source of hints and tips. Despite the friendliness and openness of everyone I met, my feelings of not belonging, of being an impostor, were gathering strength.

Another two hours and we were touching down in White-horse, Yukon Territories. The journey had taken almost thirty hours. It was a pleasant, sunny -4 degrees C and Robert Polhammer the race organiser was there to meet us. He was an understated German with a gentle face which belied the brutality of the experience he had prepared for us over the next few days.

By the time I got to the High Country Inn I felt as if the universe was conspiring to intensify my feelings of being different, isolated and inferior. Everyone appeared so relaxed, so well-equipped, so fit. I lost the comfort of my two new acquaintances and began to feel the familiar anxiety which creeps up when I'm in an unfamiliar situation and don't have someone to tell me where to be, when to be there and what to do. After I had soaked away the tension of the journey, I sat around in my room wondering what to do, watching the interminable ads for pick-up trucks on Canadian TV, missing home, and feeling very disconnected from the whole experience. I went down to the hotel restaurant in the hope of bumping into someone but didn't and returned to my room and the soothing systematic task of sorting out my sled and equipment.

It was strangely comforting when I finally met up with Col and Peter at breakfast. Familiarity is so relative in these situations. Peter had promised me some fuel for my stove which I was pleased about as it meant I wouldn't have to go searching around Whitehorse. Tom and Chris, two very experienced racers, came and checked over my gear. They gave it a general thumbs-up with slight reservations about the alkaline batteries in my head-torch (lithium batteries being better-suited to sub-zero temperatures). Tom seemed to be in his early fifties: tall, wiry and tough, with an infectious exuberance about anything to do with the race. It seemed that wherever I went in the hotel I could hear his voice, and I took him to be the stereotypical loud American. Part of me felt I should be irritated by this. I grew up in the East of Scotland, where people tend to be a bit more reserved. Even our use of language is different: careful, economical, never giving too much away. But I wasn't in the Yukon to be cautious and Tom was, in fact, immensely likeable. My respect and affection for him were to grow throughout the race.

Chris was quieter and more considered, but no less enthusiastic about racing. She was a slightly-built woman with an open and generous manner. When engaged in conversation she gave the impression of being a hundred percent present and attentive. Again, my respect for her was to grow during the event.

I killed some time wandering around Whitehorse, feeling apprehensive at the sensation of the chill air entering my nostrils and noting the strain on my calves and Achilles tendons as I crunched through the coarse, frozen snow on the uncleared sidewalks off Main Street. Whitehorse was like many small North American towns I'd seen. It reminded me of an out-of-town retail park or an industrial estate. But it seemed somehow innocent after London. The people in the shops were friendly yet appeared to be endearingly shy. The sight of groups of First Nations people congregating outside a wooden Salvation Army building, vigilant and nervous, clutching polystyrene cups of hot soup, was sad and not threatening. I longed for the familiar as I made my way back to the hotel having bought some gifts in a First Nations craft shop. I 'phoned home only to get the answering machine. I checked my watch, did the arithmetic and realized they would be in Kadiri's, the local Indian restaurant. Again I pined for the familiar, even though the torture hadn't started yet!

The whole party, comprising competitors, organizers, support staff and press, gathered in the conference room of the hotel for the pre-race meeting. This was a necessary chore involving speeches, reminders of the rules, more speeches, warnings about hazards such as overflow on the ice, animal traps (people still made a living fur-trapping here in the Yukon), moose, contaminated water, frostbite, hypothermia and bears ... so relatively straightforward! Then there were more speeches followed by a meal. Bill, an experienced dog musher, was the one speechmaker who caught and held my attention. He really knew why I was there. He spoke of the call to live an adventurous life and the quest which drives some human beings beyond the comfort zone to seek challenges and risk danger. He spoke of preparation and planning, of altering plans in response to the environment. He spoke of thinking before acting.

Many of the concepts he mentioned recalled the work I do in my other, mundane life: teaching strategies for thinking to children with a range of learning, behavioural and emotional difficulties. It was odd to hear these things spoken of in such an alien context so far removed from the classroom, yet the principles remained the same: don't panic, stop, think, assess the situation, plan, remain flexible enough to alter the plan if necessary. Bill recounted the story of a Japanese arctic explorer who found himself lost in a whiteout only yards from his tent after having stepped outside to relieve himself. He survived the night by alternately jumping up and down and lying in a shallow trench he had dug. His presence of mind enabled him to overcome panic and do what needed to be done to stay alive. I made a mental note to remember the story: I could use it with some of the pupils I worked with. Many of these were bright kids for whom school and learning were so frightening as to throw them into a panic, blocking any possibility of solving academic problems presented to them and feeding an insidious and self-fulfilling sense of themselves as failures. It was my job to provide them with strategies for managing these situations, and the Japanese explorer had just become part of my arsenal. At last, the morning of the race arrived. Time had passed slowly since leaving home, and the trials of the next few days would slow it further.

The moment has arrived. I make my way down to the Yukon River, struggling across roads with my 23 kg sled. The sun bouncing off the snow is dazzling enough to justify wearing shades without seeming pretentious. These realities knock all the pretence out of you pretty quickly, paring everything down to its most efficient and functional. I had learned that lesson during the desert race. This all seems very low key and slightly amateurish after the glamour and spectacle of the MDS, but there is a tension building nonetheless as racers gather, their sleds bumping and trekking poles tangling. A local radio man requests a few words into mic, a far cry from the media slickness of the MDS and Trans-World sport. We are herded together for a group photo and then we are off, in an anti-climax which reminds me of the start of the Thames Meander.

It feels good to be on the move as I settle in behind Col at a good, steady pace somewhere between three and four mph, according to my GPS. I note with satisfaction that the 23 kg of the sled is sliding along behind without too much effort. I hope it stays that way. We snake out of Whitehorse past a group of First Nations people drinking cheap wine in a car park on the edge of town. I feel a wave of gratitude. If I hadn't been lifted out of the life I'd been living all those years ago, who knows? I could be sitting with them. But God had other plans for me. Then it's down onto the frozen Yukon River. The trail on the river isn't so good: soft, deeply-rutted and uneven. My sled keeps pulling off-line, caught in the ruts and bumps, and I'm continually forced to yank it back in line behind me. The soft snow lying on top of the ice strains my calves and tendons with each step. This is going to be tough.

For two hours I plough on in the same way. My feet don't feel right. I stop, sit on my sled and remove my Mukluks. My army surplus Gore-Tex boot-liners are rubbing my toes, and I remove them. A mild wave of anxiety rises as I become aware of a hot-spot developing on the toes of my right foot. This is not good given that I'm only two and a half hours into a three-day race. The good news is that my feet feel better with the liners removed and the trail is firming up underfoot. I'm making good time. Col has pulled away a bit since my unscheduled stop, but I can still see him a couple of hundred metres ahead. I'm staying with him. I'm in a rhythm, covering ground well, pace steady, head down, arms pumping, trekking poles pushing me forward with a rhythmic one-two, one-two, one-two. I sing with the rhythm, taking advantage of the relative solitude to belt out a selection of Scottish folk songs. My breathing becomes laboured, and I stop singing. I had filled my hydration bladder and two thermos flasks with very hot water at the hotel. Sucking up the warm water through the bladder's drinking tube is making me feel sick. But I have to stay properly hydrated; I learned that lesson well on the Meander. I've got to be disciplined. Yeughh! I can't drink this stuff; it's turning my stomach and I may throw up. I've got to come up with a solution. I've been blowing the unused water in the tube back into the bladder to prevent it freezing up. I'm going to try leaving it in the tube to cool for a while. It'll be a balancing act, but I've got to do something. If I time it right, I'll get a cold drink before it freezes. I suck some hot water into the tube and leave it for five minutes. It works! Excellent! The nausea subsides with the first ice-cold drink, and my spirit is lifted by this small triumph.

This is a long slog on this damn river. I think back to my pace during the Snowdonia marathon and make some calculations. I figure I still have at least three hours to go before CP1. I remember the GPS which I had tucked inside my base layer to stop the batteries draining in the cold. I power it up and watch as it locks on to one, two, three then four satellites. Fantastic! I'm much nearer than I thought. I've been making excellent progress, far better than I'd expected. The GPS counts me in towards CP1. The sun is starting to go down and the Yukon sky explodes in a spectacular display of deep purples, blues, blood-reds and oranges. I am captivated and stop to breathe it in for a few moments. The awe-inspiring sight fills my heart and lifts my spirits.

I turn off the Yukon River, guided by the fluorescent green arrow spray-painted incongruously on the snow. My heart sinks again as I look up from the arrow to see Col in the near distance struggling up an impossible gradient with his sled. It seems that CP1, in the long tradition of CP locations, has been placed at the top of a 500ft cliff. I stand at the foot of the only track and survey the murderous incline.

I opt for the 'don't look at the horizon' approach, fix my gaze firmly on my feet, shorten my stride and attack. For the first time my sled becomes a real burden. My heart pounds, I breathe deep, hard and rapidly, thighs burning, head throbbing. I'm working very hard. It's a huge relief to round a bank of snow to be greeted by a smiling, clipboard-equipped race official.

She takes my number and tells me when I can leave (8:50, after the mandatory CP1, four-hour stop). That climb was a real pig after twenty-plus miles on the trail, and I'm exhausted. I make my way past a pot of stew cooking on a campfire and dump my sled in an open, treeless area. I thread my way back through the scattered sleeping racers in a variety of brightly coloured bivvy-bags and one-man tents towards the fire and a bigger tent with hot drinks inside. Someone has just dumped a load of cold water into the stew to stop it drying out so it's now cold stew. I eat a bowl anyway and drink two huge paper cups of lemon tea before heading back to sort out my sleeping gear.

I grab Robert P. He'll have to check and approve my stove and sleeping system before I can continue. I hope I get away with it. Robert has a good look, checking my improvised sleeping system (fleece liner inside a lightweight sleeping bag inside a 3-4 seasons bag inside a bag cover inside a Gore-tex bivvy-bag!).

'You won't freeze to death, but you're going to be cold'.

At least he's happy with my stove: a Swedish military thing which will burn anything. I feel a wave of shame as I look around at the other racers with their expensive, high tech, minus-50 sleeping bags. I'd had to cobble things together as best I could and had thought I'd done OK. I crawl inside my cocoon with some difficulty. I feel a certain self-satisfied smugness as I note how comfortable and warm I feel. It may not be pretty but it works just fine.

'Paul. Paul … are you awake?' I hear Col's voice pulling me out of sleep.

'I take it you're sleeping bag's OK, you've been snoring for the past two hours.'

It's 8:30. Col's decided to wait so that we can head out together on the next stage. I'm pleased about that: I didn't fancy doing it alone. The darkness and the noticeable drop in temperature make the job of packing up much more of a chore. I'm convinced I've lost something in the snow. We fill our hydration bladders and thermos flasks with hot water and drink some more lemon tea, then it's time to go, back down the incline with my sled banging into my heels (the shame makes another appearance as I compare Col's very professional-looking hired pulk-sled to my creation, fabricated out of a plastic kid's sled, some plastic plumbing pipe and a post-office mailbag).

Ten miles of a boring slog in the dark on the Yukon River. It's much colder, perhaps minus 15. The darkness makes me feel small and vulnerable; there could be all sorts of things lurking out there, just beyond the reach of my head-torch. It's harder to judge time and distance in the dark and it seems to be taking ages to reach the expected turning off the river onto the Dawson trail. We're still moving at a good pace too, nearly 4mph according to the GPS.

It's a tough climb up off the river. Steep, rough and hard to find enough traction; I keep slipping backwards. Col's strong pace never falters or slows, and he never stops to rest. I'm starting to struggle to stay with him. The trail is difficult now. After the flat of the river it has turned into small undulating hills and dips which meander through sparse coniferous woodland. The inclines are hurting my hip.

This damn hip. It feels worse this time. Every time I hit any kind of a slope it makes itself known, grinding painfully in its socket.

I'm really starting to hurt now and Col's beginning to pull away from me. I can't stay with him. I can see him waiting for me up ahead.

'I'm having big problems with my hip. I can't stay with you.'

'You were going well on the river; is it the up-hills?'

'Yeah, I can't keep this pace up.'

'I've got to keep a good pace going otherwise I seize up.' He seems almost apologetic.

'No, man, you've got to stay with your own pace. I just can't stay with you.'

'Are you sure you'll be OK?'

'Yeah, no problem, I'll plod on for a while then get my head down.'

'I'm going to try to get to CP2 in one go.'

CP1 to CP2 is around forty miles, and we've done around eighteen of those.

'There's no way I can do that; on you go, man.'

'Right, if you're sure you're OK.'

I'm embarrassed that he feels bad. Of course he's got to run his own race, that's understood. None of us would expect anything else. I don't like the thought of being out here on my own though.

I slog on for another half hour. It's a great relief to see Tom and Chris bivvying down by the side of the trail. It's 3:30am, and I'm definitely going to stop here for a while. Tom and Chris don't mind me bivvying down at the same spot. It's reassuring to be with them. I roll out my bivvy-bag in the deep snow, sinking in up to my thighs and kicking snow into my sleeping bag in the process. I'm too tired to care and fall into a deep sleep as soon as I wriggle my way into my bag.

I wake to the sound of Tom and Chris packing up. It's 5:30AM. The pair, experienced winter racers, move a few paces ahead of me, apparently effortlessly. They have a slickness and efficiency borne of years and many races together. Again the pain in my hip is constantly talking to me: 'You've got to stop, you don't have to do this. You're doing long-term damage. You can't do this.'

I'm struggling to stay with the pace again. The temperature has dropped even further: it's now around minus 20. The water in my hydration bladder has frozen in the drinking tube, despite the neoprene insulation, and I have to stop periodically to drink directly from the filler cap.

I've been struggling to stay with Tom and Chris for the past couple of hours. The water inside the insulated hydration bladder is frozen solid now too and I'm using my thermos flasks. This is forcing regular stops to go through the rigmarole of extracting the thermos from my sled to get a drink. I'm permanently playing catch up with Tom and Chris which requires a huge effort and extended periods of running with the sled. This is just another mark of my inexperience. The pain in my hip is worsening and has been joined by an old Achilles tendon injury. This is a real worry. If it goes now, my race is over. I almost want this to happen: this race has become a soul-destroying trudge. The tendon had troubled me in the latter stages of the MDS, but not like this. My anti-inflammatories seem to be having little impact on either problem.

I've got Tom and Chris in my sights again. They know I'm having issues, it's obvious. 'Good job Paul!' I would probably find this expression insufferable in any other circumstance, but Tom's encouragement and support feel genuine, and he lifts my flagging spirits. A dark shape moves in the periphery of my vision and all awareness of pain, all feelings of despondency, evaporate as I turn to witness the magnificence of a bald eagle gliding majestically towards a copse of pine trees to the left of the trail. He's less than twenty feet above me. It's a staggering, beautiful thing to witness. Tom has stopped suddenly. I feel like I should be giving him my full attention, but my heart is still with the eagle.

'Well how're we goin' to get round this?' I pull up beside him. There is a section of overflow about 40ft across and 60ft wide lying right across the trail. There is no negotiable way around. We try, but it ends with Tom putting his foot through the ice into freezing water. It's the first time I've heard him curse. The overflow is frozen, but there's no way of telling how strong it is. Still we'll have to cross it.

'It looks risky Tom.' It's a pointless thing to say.

'That's why you're here, isn't it?'

I'm reminded of Bill's speech: a hazard like this requires certain precautions. I watch Tom and Chris pull on their Neos, which are multi-layer Gore-Tex over-boots. I feel embarrassed as I pull two plastic rubble sacks over my Mukluks and secure them with army surplus arctic gaiters, another of my cobbled-together solutions. Again, it's not pretty, but I think it will work well if I go through the ice.

Tom's across OK, but there's nothing I can do as Chris loses her footing on the shiny surface and crashes to the ice with a dull thud. The impact sends out a spider web of cracks, but the ice holds.

It's my turn. The ice creaks beneath me as I make my way gingerly out to the middle like a new-born deer trying to find its feet. I can see flat bubbles of trapped air searching for ways out as I cross the cracked section where Chris went down. I feel exhilarated as I reach the far side of the overflow. According to the recently-arrived skidoo driver, there are several more sections of overflow to cross today. In any case it took my mind off the pain in my hip for a while. Tom and Chris have stopped ahead for a drink. They did this race last year.

'We must be near the start of the big climb into CP2: you've got about ten miles of hard climb into the checkpoint.'

My heart sinks. 'I'm struggling guys.'

Chris gives me a concerned smile. My struggle has been obvious. Tom looks me in the eye. 'You're almost halfway, you've used nothing like half of the time allocation. This is a 72-hour race: use them all if you have to. You can do this.'

The time has come, inevitably I guess, when I fall behind again. It's just like the Thames Meander, falling further and further back. I'm useless at these things, weaker than everybody else. Who the hell do I think I'm kidding? Tom's words are encouraging, practical words to leave me with but I'm finding them hard to hear. Chris takes a photo, wishes me well and thrusts a packet of beef jerky into my hand. Tom and Chris disappear around a bend in the trail and on into the woodland which seems to be getting denser after the sparse and patchy, stunted pines of the past few hours. I'm not convinced that in their hearts they really believe I'll make it. I start into the climb on my own. My hip and tendon hurt like hell and I'm already over my limit with the anti-inflammatories.

I've managed an hour of climbing but I've got to stop. I struggle to extricate my bivvy bag from the sled and roll it out, stumbling and cursing in the knee-deep snow. I fight my way into the bag and fall instantly into a deep sleep.

I am woken by the warmth of a bright sun on my face, filtered pink through the red Gore-Tex of my bivvy-bag. I hear the 2-stroke rasp of a skidoo in the near distance, shattering the tranquillity of the place. I pack up slowly, stiffly and painfully.

'How ya doin'?'

The driver's not officially part of the race but a co-opted

Whitehorse resident who had been returning from Braeburn, further up the trail.

'I'm struggling, man. I don't know if I can do this.'

My spirits are at their lowest yet as I recount the litany of aches, pains and injuries.

'There's another skidoo on its way down from Braeburn. He should be with you in about twenty minutes if you want to scratch. You don't want to mess your hip up long-term.'

He looks at the notoriously inaccurate odometer on the skidoo.

'You've got around seven miles to go 'til the checkpoint.'

That translates to around three hours, maybe even four at my current pace. I'm only getting slower.

'Good luck.' The skidoo belches a black 2-stroke cloud and lurches off past an approaching racer. This guy looks like he's out for a stroll in the park. I hook up with this delightfully good-humoured Englishman. He reminds me of the stereotypical English eccentric, composed and cheerful regardless of circumstance or adversity. I feel like a dour, miserable Scot next to him. I half-expect him to pull out a china tea set and some cucumber sandwiches (with the crusts removed) each time we stop. But this guy is tough. Underneath the refined, gentle exterior is a very determined and self-sufficient individual. He sets his own pace and won't deviate from it. Surprisingly, I'm actually moving a little faster than him and I stop less. I'm going to press on.

The climb to CP2 seems interminable. I've lost track of the time but seven miles was way out. It's tough going too. Uphill all the way and rough underfoot.

I'm out of water. Absolutely nothing left. This is not good. I'm working hard and need liquid. This is a lonely, miserable stretch, and I don't like covering ground in the dark. I turn the crisp air blue with my curses and wince at the sickening pain in my hip each time I miss my footing, or slip, or step into snow which is deeper than expected.

Wait! I smell a faint whiff of woodsmoke. I round a bend in the trail and emerge into a clearing. There it is: CP2 on a rise overlooking the ominously named Dog Grave Lake. The checkpoint is a sorry-looking orange canvas wall tent but there is smoke coming from a metal chimney pipe and that means a stove, warmth and rest.

I feel no elation, merely exhausted relief. I dump my sled and crouch, stiffly, in under the tent flap. The small tent is crowded but warm.

There's a slight air of panic here. Something is wrong. Bundled in one corner is what appears to be a pile of sleeping bags and down jackets. My God! It's Tom! He's in a very bad way. I get the story from the race official. He'd become progressively sicker as he and Chris climbed towards CP2. He had been unable to eat or drink nearly enough. In spite of having drunk very little he'd been urinating copiously. His body was rebelling and something was deeply wrong. Now, despite the mound of sleeping bags, down jackets and hot shot heat pads inside the bags, he's getting colder. Tom is in trouble. It'll take several hours, a very rough skidoo ride, followed by more hours in an ambulance before he'll reach Whitehorse and the nearest hospital. Chris won't be continuing either. She's going to stay with Tom.

I sit on an upturned sled by the stove and shovel down chicken and blackbean stew along with several large paper mugs of the omnipresent lemon tea. I claim a corner and crawl into my bag.

I have never felt so physically and mentally defeated. The nearest I've come to this was the long stage during the MDS. Now I had to contend with injury, solitude and the miserable, unrelenting cold, which made the simplest of tasks a soul-destroying chore. I overhear the race official who has just checked the thermometer outside the tent. 'Minus thirty, ladies and gentlemen!' She is a local and seems to be enjoying the suffering of us incomers. I feel like crying and my throat tightens up as I fight the tears back. It would not be cool to burst into tears. I've already told the official that I'm not sure I can go on. She seemed to find this quite satisfying, or maybe I'm just becoming paranoid. I'm not going to make a final decision until I've had some sleep. Again, Bill's speech influences my choices.

I sleep fitfully, waking often to resume the wrestling match with myself. I can't go on, I'm finished, the pain is just too much. People back home would understand. I'm *injured*. Nobody could blame me. But how could I face my family and friends if I quit? I never quit. My whole life as far back as I can remember has been about not quitting, not giving up. I've struggled and held on, and toughed my way through all manner of adversity. I'd battled and recovered from a drink problem; I'd hung in there in a marriage which was often difficult and painful. How would I live with myself if I sacked now? Too much of my whole idea of who I am rests on finishing this race. *I can't quit*. But that's just stupid talk. It hurts too much. I can't make it. Maybe this is not who I am. I'm so, so tired. And so it goes, for hours.

It's around 2am. I awake to the sound of a vaguely familiar voice. It's Shona, but she sounds strange. Her words are slurred and she's rambling, remonstrating with the race official about something. I know Shona from the Meander and the MDS and I've spoken to her a number of times in recent weeks in her capacity as a promoter of this event through the adventure racing website. She even lent me the bivvy-bag to help keep my costs down. I know that although she's an experienced endurance athlete she's not at her happiest in these cold weather events. I'd seen her at the start-line and I'd had my concerns then as she seemed overdressed. Most racers start the race in only a base layer and a fleece and/or windproof layer, which is adequate in the milder early stages. But poor Shona really feels the cold and she seemed to be wearing everything she had, right up to her heavy down jacket. As the race developed she had become more and more tired and progressively chilled until her core body temperature had fallen dangerously low. Shona and her partner had bivvied down by the trail in an attempt to get warm, but could not maintain their core temperature. Crucially for them both, Shona had hired a satellite 'phone and had been able to call for help. Had this not been the case, the consequences for both of them could have been fatal. By the time the skidoo reached them, both were hypothermic and Shona was barely conscious. Now they are wrapped in down sleeping bags by the stove, being fed hot drinks and waiting while Tom is evacuated. Hot food and the relative warmth of the tent have worked their magic and they are warming up. Shona is gradually returning to her formidable self as she waits her turn for the long skidoo ride out of danger.

I return to my own personal battle. No nearer a resolution, I drift again into a fitful sleep.

I wake with a start. It's 5am. I try rotating my foot deep in the warmth of my sleeping bag. The tendon feels tight and sore. My hip still clicks and grinds sickeningly in its socket. What the hell should I do? I can't bear the thought of going home having failed. How many times would I have to recount the tale of how I didn't make it? What would happen about the sponsor money raised for the NSPCC? But the thought of continuing is equally dreadful.

I know from past dilemmas and impasses that the torture of indecision will only end with action. Before I have the chance to change my mind, I tell the official I'll be leaving at dawn. I eat and drink as much as I can while my Mukluks sit by the stove until they thaw out and become supple enough to get back on my feet.

I leave CP2 just as dawn is tugging at the blanket of darkness. Apparently during the same dark troubled night I had spent battling with myself in this terrible, beautiful place, the Yukon sky had been lit up with a spectacular display of the Northern Lights. It feels symbolic of something that I missed them. All beauty or semblance of pleasure is now lost on me. It just hurts, all the time. I root around in my waist pouch for anti-inflammatories. I find one and a bit. I swallow them and plough on, soon drawing up behind a German racer, Pieter, and Lynda, a local racer. Catching them lifts my spirits a little as they had left CP2 some time before me. Their pace suits me well, especially as they build in occasional stops. These are essential for me now as my hydration bladder is still frozen solid. No great surprise as it's below minus 30 now! There's no doubt about it, this place could kill you. Ice is crystallizing on my beard, moustache and eyebrows, and even on my eyelashes. As I struggle forward, the pain builds again and I sink into a dark mental pit. My weakened, vulnerable state invites a vicious and familiar little troll onto my shoulder. He assails me with every painful event he can conjure from my past. Every hurt, every betrayal, every humiliation is played out in my mind in glorious technicolour. Every emotional wound, whatever the stage of healing, is worried open again and the troll sits there laughing.

The pain in my hip jolts me back to the moment and I trudge miserably on. I use the anger to push me forward.

The race official at CP2, a local wilderness guide, had mentioned a hunter's shack about fifteen miles along the trail. It will be open and there's a rudimentary stove so we'll be able to melt some snow and re-fill our flasks. She said that the shack appears a short way after the trail widens out. Apparently, you can't miss it.

This is crazy. It's been a long, tough slog. Six, maybe seven hours. Still no sign of a widening in the trail, never mind a shack. I don't understand it. Neither do Pieter and Lynda. Maybe we have missed it. We've been making good speed according to my GPS. We should be very close to the shack.

The tell-tale two-stroke rasp announces the arrival of a skidoo and the driver slides to a halt in the deeper snow at the edge of the trail. The two-stroke fumes are made doubly offensive by their contrast with the clean, cold air.

'How far to the shack?'

'Oh, maybe a couple of miles. Everybody OK?'

It's a stupid question under the circumstances, but we all nod anyway.

Now it's been an hour's hard grind since we spoke to the skidoo man. What's going on? Where is this damned shack? Now I can hear a two-stroke engine again, more than one. It's Shona and her partner being evacuated. Robert P is driving the first skidoo. He informs us that there are still another seven miles to go before we get to the shack.

What the hell is going on? These people don't know what

they're talking about. I'm sick of the mind games. If they're not sure about the distances, they should keep their mouths shut. I am raging. This is difficult enough without this bullshit, and I can't disguise my anger.

Robert attempts to diffuse the situation.

'Come on guys, you know it's always like this in these races. It's difficult to gauge distances, they always seem longer than they really are.'

This doesn't make me feel any better. Sure, it's hard to judge distances, but this is blatant misinformation, either from these guys or the previous skidoo man. It probably doesn't seem so important when you're sitting on a skidoo. But in my current condition this news is hard to take. I'm reminded of the scene in *Ice Cold in Alex* when the four main characters have spent the whole day in the baking desert sun, hand-cranking a truck in reverse to the top of a huge sand dune, only for it to roll all the way back down just as they are reaching the top.

Pieter's morale has taken a real nosedive since the news about the shack. His feet are in a mess and he's been in a lot of pain since CP2. It hasn't slowed his pace until now but the frustration and disappointment of believing the shack was just around the corner, and then having to grind through another three or four hours has hit him hard. His head's gone down, along with his pace.

It's weird, but I'm feeling quite strong again. It's very strange and I don't really understand it. Even the pain doesn't seem so bad. Lynda has decided to plough on to the shack and get the stove going. I guess it's up to me to encourage, bully and cajole Pieter along until he gets through this bad patch. This guy really is suffering. I dread to think what state his feet are in. He's wearing heavy boots, like the ones arctic oil-rig workers wear. They've got him crippled. I had nearly opted for a pair of those myself. Lucky escape.

And there it is. Like a garden shed dropped from heaven. I never thought it possible to be so overjoyed by the sight of a 10ft by 10ft shed. I'd almost given up on it. We've both been smelling phantom woodsmoke for the past two hours. Seven miles from the skidoo is probably about right. It has taken around ten hours of brutal, heads-down slog to get to this place from CP2.

What have we got? A couple of plywood bunks and a dodgy old stove. It might as well be the Ritz Hotel. We take turns sawing wood for the stove and melting snow to re-fill vacuum flasks. I treat myself to a foil packed ready-meal of vegetable curry, heated in a pot of boiling water. This is my first hot food since CP2, and it's fantastic. I wolf it down as Pieter takes a knife to his infected, ruined feet. I throw a bottle of iodine in his direction: he'll need it. I lie down on the floor of the shack on a length of grimy foam rubber. Too tired to wrestle my sleeping bag out of my sled, I zip up my down jacket and painfully drag off my mukluks. It feels good to liberate my aching feet as I turn my toes upwards and push my heels down, stretching out the offending tendon. This action had eased the pain a little at CP2, and I hope it does the same again as I'm long since out of painkillers.

I wake with a start after what seems like a few minutes. It has been about an hour. Lynda is shuffling around, packing for the off. We've been joined by Kev who'd left CP2 shortly after me. His feet are a painful mess too.

It takes us less than ten minutes until we're ready to go, I'm getting good at this. It's dark outside and very cold. My head torch gave up the ghost last night, the life sucked out of the batteries by the cold. Lynda suggests Kev lend me his spare. For some reason I'm not so sure about this. I don't want to be beholden to anyone. This is a familiar feeling. I shouldn't really need a torch anyway, there are several other people and I'll be able to follow without one. But maybe I'm being stupid. The torch has been offered; it would be churlish not to take it. I'll take it.

Kev has made a request not to go at the back. I'm really not sure about this. He's struggling because of his feet and he's by far the slowest of the four of us. Our natural pace is going to be too much for him. If they agree to his request - and that's exactly what appears to be happening - that puts me at the back, behind him! That will drag me further and further back. I'm not having it.

While this is being discussed I make my position clear and drag my sled past him. There is a bad vibe in the air and the previous harmony has been punctured. Kev is not happy about me pushing past. Pieter is clearly concerned about Kev's weakened condition too. I feel fear. I'm struggling here. I'm cold, I'm in pain, and I'm tired. I want this thing to be over. I don't want to be held up by anybody else. Yes, maybe it is selfish. Maybe I should have more compassion. Maybe it is ruthless even. I don't care. This guy just won't take responsibility for himself. I haven't asked any quarter, why should I give any? What does he want us to do, carry him to the finish line?

'We made an agreement to stay together, Paul.'

'Don't give me that, Kev. You made the agreement, not me.'

It's getting childish now and I'm getting angry. I hate being pushed around or manipulated.

'OK, Paul, but if you start to leave me behind, I want my head-torch back.'

I get all Scottish - my default position when the pressure is on - and tell Kev precisely and directly what he can do with his torch. Lynda is between us now, hands outstretched like a boxing referee. She's trying to calm things down. She motions to me to hang on to the torch and I turn away.

I've had an hour or so to think. The reality is that I am afraid. I'm exhausted, injured and struggling. Kev is mirroring my 'weakness' back to me just a bit too closely for comfort. I don't want to be left behind because that would terrify me, and I don't know if I could make it on my own. But that's what I was going to do to him. I didn't give a damn. I just didn't want him holding me up. I feel guilty and ashamed at my callousness.

We're forced to stop every fifteen minutes or so for Kev to catch up. The truth is that I welcome the stops. I can rest for a couple of minutes and the pain in my hip and tendon ease a little in those precious moments of respite as we wait for him to shuffle up behind. Every time he catches up, he thanks us. I feel worse every time he says it. Here he comes again. His feet are ruined and he's a sorry sight. This guy climbed Denali a couple of years back. That's a serious mountain. You've just got to respect that. I look at him, trying not to shine the head-torch in his face. He's really suffering. I offer him my hand and he takes it.

'I'm sorry I gave you such a hard time back there, Kev. I'm struggling too.'

'It's OK, man. We're all tired.'

He's cold. 'Have you got anything warm to drink, Kev?'

'No. I've got plenty of water, but it's cold.'

I've long since stopped worrying about the taste of warm water. My body welcomes the warmth now, and there's not a hint of nausea.

'Get some of this down you.' I give him a drink from my thermos and he takes it gratefully and graciously.

We've settled into a steady pattern. We stop every hour, on the hour, for five minutes to rest and drink. We've managed to keep this up for four hours and even with the pauses for Kev we're going really well, trudging our way through sparse coniferous woodland. Now the head-torches keep catching on something fluorescent and orange up ahead. Excellent! It's the '10 miles to CP3' marker. We celebrate with a drink stop. I shout the good news back to Kev who's shuffling along a little way back. A wave of jubilation passes through our little band. But the pleasure of the moment passes quickly. Ten miles is ten miles. At this pace, we're talking about another five hours at least. I don't voice my thoughts. I'm still feeling ashamed at my display of mean-spirited negativity back at the hunter's shack.

The trail is narrowing now and the trees are getting taller. The woodland has become a forest, forming dense, high walls on either side of us. My head-torch (Kev's head-torch!?) penetrates barely a few feet into the green blackness. There are plenty of animal tracks criss-crossing the trail, more than anywhere else so far. They disappear into the darkness occasionally and then re-appear further up the trail. It's unnerving. Those are definitely moose tracks, while the small ones could be lynx. The broad, close-together ones could be wolverine. I dread to think what made the huge, round ones with the 4ft stride. I keep telling myself they look quite old, maybe even a few days. But listen to me: all of a sudden I'm Geronimo! Let's face it: I know nothing about this stuff. Apparently, it's best to make a noise so you don't catch any wildlife by surprise. I bang my trek poles together and loudly enquire after Kev's wellbeing. I hope my sad efforts at scaring the bears away are not too obvious to the others. I'm a kid from an Edinburgh council estate, it's two in the morning and I'm in the middle of a forest full of grizzly bears in the heart of the Yukon Territories. I smile nervously at the absurdity of my situation.

I'm bored now. This forest trail has gone on for hours: interminable, dreary, unchanging, exhausting hours.

The approaching rasp of a skidoo breaks through the monotony.

'Two miles to go across the lake, but it's a real tough finish. I'll park the skidoo up at the fork in the trail and light your way down onto the lake.'

Here we go. The trail down onto the lake is steep and precarious. Suddenly my sled careers past me, knocking me off my feet and dragging me helplessly down the steep, icy slope … the 'quick way down'!

We're all on the lake now except Kev, who's gone missing. We did wait at the top of the slope for ages but he didn't show. OK, so the guy's struggling, but this is driving me nuts. We're so close. What the hell does he want from us? The skidoo man has gone back to check on him. Pieter has had enough of waiting; he's headed off on his own. Lynda is feeling guilty but wants to get moving too; it's cold out here in the middle of this lake and we're both seizing up.

I don't feel guilty enough to hang around. I wait until I see Kev's head-torch slithering down the trail onto the lake, then I head off. Lynda's had enough too and seems satisfied now that Kev's out of the woods. We'll send the skidoo man to check on him when we get in to the finish.

But the truth is that none of us are 'out of the woods' yet. The trail up off the lake is a nightmare. It really is a sick joke that the steepest, most difficult terrain of the whole race should come now, within a mile of the finish. I drag myself up powdery slopes, slipping backwards all the time. My heart feels frighteningly close to the limits of its functioning. I remember the heartbreaking struggle to get to the top of the high dunes on the long stage of the MDS, and the soul-destroying frustration as the dunes crumbled more rapidly the nearer we got to the apex. The despair of being dragged back down as we scrambled on all fours, knee deep in sand. The same soul-destroying, energy-sapping, infuriating battle is playing out right here in the snow. Again, I'm scrabbling on all fours, this time grabbing at low branches, exposed roots, anything to drag myself and this damned sled to the top of each incline.

Mercifully that hellish section ends after only a quarter of a mile or so. Now it's a straightforward walk in to the finish. Lynda and I emerge from the trees and out of the darkness into a huge floodlit clearing. It's a spectacular anti-climax: a ramshackle collection of wooden buildings and outbuildings, a caravan, a couple of pickup trucks, a rusty engine block, a steering column, a Harley in a shed waiting for summer, and a barking dog. So this is Braeburn truck-stop, the end of the torture. The utilitarian looking wooden building with the lights on is showing the most signs of life. It feels good to unharness this damn sled for the last time and dump it unceremoniously in the dirty snow of the car-park. I climb a short flight of stairs and walk inside.

The proprietor is a bear of a man with a huge grey beard, a belly to match and hands like snow shovels (I suspect he may be the owner of the Harley). It's 4AM but he's serving enormous burgers to a motley collection of exhausted 'racers' (I guess we've all earned the title). I rouse the sleeping skidoo man and inform him of Kev's predicament. He drags himself out of his sleeping bag without complaint and prepares to head out into the cold night once again. Lynda goes with him. Her guilt has got the better of her and she's planning to walk Kev in to the finish. I just can't figure that woman out. What is it that drives some women to behave like this? Why do they have to have somebody to care-take? Why the hell do I care so much? I'm irritated but I'm also aware of a nagging feeling of guilt. She's doing something I couldn't do. I'd shoved my way past Kev at the shack in order to look after myself. I don't know if I was right or wrong to do that. I do know that I feel ashamed of it and now, to make myself feel better, I'm judging Lynda's actions harshly. It isn't working. I don't feel better.

So that's it. No crowds. No banners. No medal or embrace from the race director. Just a 'well done' from the lone race official, a 'Braeburn special' burger and a cup of coffee. I find a grotty mattress on the floor of a grotty room with posters of naked women on the walls and a smell of wet dogs (or maybe that's me). I slip instantly into a deep, dreamless sleep. Robert, the race director, gingerly pokes his head around the door at around 8am, presumably anticipating the violent reception he had predicted on the trail. 'Congratulations, we leave for Whitehorse in 15 minutes.'

In the truck *en route* to Whitehorse, Robert enquires about my injuries. News travels fast in these parts! I joke about quitting this kind of race and taking up 'extreme knitting' or maybe 'adventure baking', perhaps even 'ultra crochet' instead. Behind the jokes and the laughter, I'm genuinely worried about the shape I'm in and a little ashamed of my 'weakness.'

Above all, I'm glad it's over.

CHAPTER 9

Mirror, Mirror, On the Wall

WHEN I SAW Col in the foyer of the High Country Inn I knew immediately, from the expression on his face, that he thought I hadn't made it. Sure enough, he'd been told by the lone official at Braeburn that I had scratched at CP2. Chinese whispers, I guess. I raged inside when I heard this. I had just pushed my body, mind and spirit further than I'd ever done in my life, and I'd made it. I'd finished this beast of a race, the toughest thing I'd ever done. Now I'd discovered that, from the comfort of her cosy little spot in the diner at the Braeburn truck-stop, someone who wasn't even out on the trail was telling people I'd quit. I never quit! It felt like she'd stolen something from me, something very precious. Col's face lit up when I put him straight on this point. When he'd last seen me I had been in bad shape, and he could be forgiven for believing that I hadn't made it. It had been him who'd asked the official at Braeburn if there was any news about me.

I dumped my stinking gear in my hotel room and thanked God that I'd gone for the Jacuzzi bath option when I'd booked over the 'phone from England. I eased my aching, battered body gingerly into the steaming water and hit the button. I

145

luxuriated blissfully in the bubbling water and allowed it to wash over me for two hours before limping back downstairs to meet Col for lunch.

We ate monster steaks and drank buckets of Coke, thus beginning the long process of putting back some of what we'd taken out of our bodies over the previous few days. We talked through the race, recounting events from the point at which we'd separated. Col's biggest problem had been hallucinations brought on by sleep deprivation. He'd ploughed on with the absolute minimum of sleep and during the forest section before the last lake crossing his mind had started to play games. The sound of his sled grinding in the snow behind him had morphed into the heavy, grunting breath of a bear which he'd become convinced was following him. He'd slipped in and out of this sleep-deprived madness for hours in those woods, and he'd been alone.

It had been a brutal race, miserable even. The Marathon des Sables had stretched me way beyond what I thought I was capable of, but this had been something altogether different. There had of course been highs and lows on the MDS, but for me the Yukon had been a series of lows and lowers. There had been none of the evening camaraderie of the bivouac, none of the mandatory overnight stops, where my body could begin to repair itself. This harsh place had none of the exotic romance of the desert. It had been brutal, lonely, cold, painful endurance all the way. Yes, I had finished it, but I felt no elation. No great sense of pride or achievement, not even the quiet satisfaction of the days following the MDS. All I knew at this point was that the suffering had stopped, and for that I was truly grateful. 'Toughest and coldest' … absolutely.

I knew more about myself than I'd done a few days

previously. I didn't like everything I'd learned. The race had broken me. My ego had been weakened to the extent that some kind of grace could appear. I'd come up hard against aspects of my personality which, in my 'other', mundane existence, I could skilfully evade or even deny the very existence of. Here in the Yukon those same traits had been raw and obvious. The thin, dissipated Arctic light had exposed my shadow with even greater clarity than had the intensity of the desert sun.

I wasn't proud of the man who had projected his own fears and weaknesses onto Kev with such a callous absence of compassion. I was embarrassed by the childish intensity of my reaction on discovering that the race official had been informing people that I had quit. Somewhere along the line I had lost my connection with mission and purpose. Spirit hadn't stopped guiding me, I'd just stopped listening. I'd been taking all my directions from my ego instead. I had hated the thought of people believing I'd failed. It seems weak and immature to be so concerned about what people think of me. I struggled, and indeed still struggle, with this stuff. My lack of compassion for Kev reflects a deep-rooted lack of compassion for myself. Nothing I do is ever enough. No matter what I achieve, there's a harsh, critical little troll living under some bridge inside my head, just waiting to steal all my gold. He's the same parasitic, mean little creature who whispers in my ear that I must do twice as much as everyone else in order to feel half as worthwhile, because I'm not good enough. It seems that somewhere, way down deep, I have a core belief about myself which says that I'm not attractive, I'm not lovable, I'm not OK. If I am to be approved of, if I am to be accepted, if I am to be loved, then I must earn it through pain.

I recall a pivotal experience in my life. I had been about

thirteen years old. I was halfway through my two-bus journey to school and was sitting on a low wall at the bus stop at the top of Lady Road waiting for the number 42 to arrive. A few metres away stood a girl from the same year group as me. She wasn't one of the 'super cool', 'super gorgeous', 'super popular' girls, but she was pretty, slight and feminine. I had never spoken to her. I looked at her with a profound longing in my heart. I felt tears fill my eyes and a tightness in my throat. I wanted to hold her, to put my arms around her. I was overcome with a deep, acutely painful sadness. In that instant I took on board a message that would play and play in my head for many years to come. 'No-one like her will ever want me,' the silent voice shouted in my ear. Whatever this 'thing' was that I so longed for, I was never going to have it: this human connection, this love and warmth - it would never be mine. I didn't understand why, but somehow I 'knew' that I didn't deserve it. I 'knew' I was not attractive or lovable. I 'knew' I was on my own. Anything good in life would come as a reward for carrying the weight of this 'knowledge'. I was destined to struggle.

This was a powerful message indeed, and a heavy one for a 13-year-old to carry. Looking back, it seems so obvious that this was one of many examples where feminine beauty gives a potent sign of transcendence; a metaphor for the true object of my longing; the love which resides in the ultimate source of mercy and compassion. What I yearned for was the Beloved. But it was far from obvious then.

The voice is still there and it still tells me that it's not who I am that matters, not even what I do. This voice, the voice of the troll, insists that it's the level of suffering I can endure that really matters, and I'm not just talking about racing. When I'm really up against it, this severe inner voice, this savage little judge, projects outwards onto anyone who passes too close. That's why Kev got it. I thought I'd dealt with the troll. I thought I'd cut him down to size. But he's still in there, on the treadmill, in training for his next appearance.

So, what's in it for me? Why do I persist with this way of thinking? The troll is a part of me after all. Part of me is clinging to this belief system. What would I have to give up if I let go of the need to endure, the need to struggle and push myself to the edge in this way? It has become my 'identity'. I'm the guy who endures, whether in races or in life. I can do it. I can endure suffering. It somehow keeps me 'special'. If I let go of that 'identity', what will I be left with? I might disappear altogether. Yet there is good news sitting quietly behind all this noise: I wasn't born with these beliefs about myself. I acquired them along the way, I learned them. If that's true, then I can unlearn them and replace them with something more useful, something more beautiful.

Shadow. It is always there, lurking in the wings. The God of the Wild Places shines a spotlight on those parts of me which, under normal circumstances, would remain in the murk doing their clandestine work. The light drains them of some of their power to trip me up, just as the cold had drained the power from my batteries. But there's something else, something important. The shadow stuff isn't always dark, or 'bad'. I also body-swerve and deny the 'Gold'. An experience like The Yukon Arctic Ultra puts a lot into perspective with regard to what I think I can or can't do. It's impossible to deny the tenacity and discipline which pushed me on after my 'dark night of the soul' at CP2. No matter how hard I try to wriggle out of owning those qualities I'm left with the fact that it did take courage to go back out on the trail that morning. I don't think I'm alone when I say that owning the 'Gold' feels less comfortable, less natural, than owning the darker, less attractive aspects of who I am.

Things start to get really complicated when I consider the dark shadow of my tenacity and discipline; I can and do use them to punish myself. The mean little troll gets in the driving seat once again, takes hold of all that beautiful tenacity and steely discipline and drives me into the ground with it. 'If it's not hurting you it's no good,' he reminds me. 'You deserve all this pain, get on with it. Or are you going to wimp out and run away like you did from that fight when you were nine?'

It's all too easy for me to default to that setting. Shadow is a slippery business. One second I think I've spotted it, the next it has gone again. I have been blessed with strong and perceptive friends who love me enough to point unflinchingly at my shadow when it does show up.

I'd also learned a good deal about my body in the Yukon, although 'body' doesn't adequately describe what I mean. At times during the race, when I was near what I thought was my limit, I found myself – my ego? – negotiating with some other part of me: not my body, exactly, but something else. My body seemed more like a collection of parts working together, like a machine, directed by this 'other'. It seems that this 'machine' has two modes in which it operates. There's the everyday mode which gets me around and enables me to function in the world. While operating in this mode it will tolerate a considerable amount of punishment and exertion. During events like the Thames Meander, the Marathon des Sables and the Yukon Arctic Ultra I'd pushed my body far beyond the limits of that mode. On the other side of some invisible line there commences a battle between mind and body.

Let's take the Yukon race as an example. I was asking too

much and my body was screaming its complaint, insisting that I stop and allow it to rest and repair. In order to make its point it flooded me with pain, fatigue, depression and anxiety. There seems, however, to be another mode, a survival mode if you like. This mode holds a remarkable reserve of strength, energy and focus. Unfortunately, it doesn't want me to know it's there and certainly won't give itself up easily. This mode is strictly for emergencies. At some point during the Yukon ordeal (maybe half-way to the hunter's shack), the 'other' part of me, the part which gives the orders to my body, seemed to acknowledge that the situation was serious. Its job changed from being an all-out campaign aimed at stopping me, into a mission to get me the hell out of there to somewhere safe. The pain was blocked to a manageable level, my focus sharpened. I could feel each mouthful of food that I consumed being transformed within seconds into useable energy, warming my body and urging my spent legs onwards. The worst part was the gap between the two modes. They did not run seamlessly, one into the other. For many miles before CP2 and for many miles after, I had been moving forwards on bloody-mindedness alone, dredging up resentments, hurts, humiliations and anger from years past and using their energy to bully my pleading limbs into continuing. During that dreadful gap it had been up to me to give the orders.

Throughout the Marathon des Sables, preparation, race and post-race, I had felt as though I was 'slaying dragons'. Of course, it had been tough, but I had been liberated and energised by the whole experience. The Yukon Arctic Ultra had been a dark descent, like plummeting through the ice into a shadowy underworld of fear and pain to do battle with demons. Both experiences had a value beyond price.

The problem with my hip and Achilles tendon didn't subside in the weeks following the race. After a month or so I decided I had better do something about it. As luck (or fate!) would have it, the consultant who checked me out was a runner. An ultra-runner at that and a veteran of the Comrades ultra and the Two Oceans race as well as many other marathons. He took one look at my x-rays and knew exactly what the problem was. It seemed that I had extra spurs of bone protruding from both my left hip and my right Achilles tendon. As my joints became inflamed during the race, the tendons running down the outside of my leg had been snagging on the spur and the more inflamed it had become the more savagely it snagged, and the more painful it became. A similar scenario had been playing out on my right heel. The X-rays also confirmed that the problem with my foot after the Snowdonia marathon had been caused by a 'greenstick' fracture sustained in the latter stages of the race.

I was referred for a course of physiotherapy. The physiotherapist inquired as to what had precipitated the problem with my hip. I gave her a brief resume. 'What the hell do you expect?' came her impressively frank reply. She knew her job, and four months of therapy got me back out on the roads again with a manageable level of discomfort. She informed me that if I did the right stretches and core stability work my hip wouldn't necessarily get worse, but that it was unlikely to get any better either. She also reassured me that just because it hurts when I run, this doesn't necessarily mean I'm doing any further damage. I hope she's right.

A couple of months after my return from the Yukon I clicked open the YAU newsletter. I read through the results table and began to peruse the race reports. My eye settled on the story of how Lynda had 'brought two racers to the finish line before returning to help a third.' I was furious. I felt wounded, as though someone had sneaked into my castle and stolen my treasure. Nobody had 'brought' me to any finish line. I'd got there under my own steam and it had taken every last ounce of resolve I could dredge up to do it. I'd sent a furious e-mail to Robert, the race director, before I realised what was happening. My shadows were out to play. My little troll-critic had hijacked me again, and he wasn't letting go yet.

CHAPTER 10

The Red Road

THE EVENTS OUTLINED in these pages describe a process of initiation and waystations *en route* to finding a home for my spirit. Before these events I was, in many respects, still a boy, and certainly lost. I became aware of the need for change. I came to a point of clear intention. I took action, and the God of the Wild Paces came to my aid. Over many years He'd sent His angels to whisper tales of adventure in my ear and I was always the hero at the heart of the action. Eventually I heard their voices. I responded to the Call and was transformed. I had spent years waiting for my 'real life' to begin, biding my time, poised for the big lightning-bolt of inspiration to strike and fix everything. I had twisted and contorted myself to fit the role I'd been assigned, seeking security and approval. But this had never worked. The inspiration came only when I literally put one foot in front of the other and embarked on my Quest, risking failure and humiliation, risking success and all the uncertainty and expectation that might come with it.

I have spoken much about shadow and the messages and 'identities' I picked up in the early part of my journey through life. I mistakenly believed that it was all down to me. I created a belief system that said that life, for me, was always going to be tough. I believed I would have to suffer for anything worthwhile and that a price would be exacted for every inch of progress I made through life. That was the only way I could become worthy to receive anything good. I dragged the burden of these erroneous, counter-productive messages with me into manhood and they gathered weight along the way.

In my twenties I had stopped drinking and the real journey began. Aged thirty-six I reached deep down inside and pulled and dragged and spat and puked out that dark cargo. I accepted the messy task of pulling it apart and took a long, hard, close-up look at it. Then, aged thirty-eight, I strapped it onto my back and headed out across the desert. Next, I packed its weight in a sled and dragged it through the Yukon. What my heart truly longed for had, of course, always been there, veiled by layers of ego and self-centred fear. The next and greatest adventure was the lifting of those veils and the removal of all the idols I had accumulated. I had resisted the call of Islam for fifteen years: reading books and talking to wise people, but at the same time turning my face away from the many signs which were placed before me. Then, when the cycle had again reached a nadir, my ego once again subdued by the trials which life placed before me, I could resist the truth no longer. I made the trip to an Islamic retreat in Norfolk where a Sheikh took my hand and heard my *Shahada*, the Islamic profession of faith:

> *'ašhadu 'an lā 'ilāha 'illa'llāhu, wa-'ašhadu 'anna
> Muhammadan rasūlu'llāh'*

> *'I bear witness that there is no deity except Allah and I
> bear witness that Muhammad is the messenger of Allah'*

When this weight was lifted from my heart it left a space for something else to flow into: something new and creative, some compassion, maybe even some love.

The transformation I speak of isn't a 'once and for all' isolated event, something to be completed, a box ticked, the experience filed. The energy at work was, and is, the energy of initiation. Initiation is an ongoing process, not an event. Like some sixteenth-century gold-seeking adventurer, I have embarked on a fantastic voyage, and while I can disembark in various exotic locations, admire the view, learn a thing or two and maybe even pick up some scars, while I live, the voyage itself never ends. After that, God alone knows my spirit's destination.

Initiation is cyclical. It is a process of continuous renewal, a circle of regeneration. I am energised and excited by the possibilities of the adventure. I am also aware that with the new vistas over the horizon there will inevitably be a challenge. This scares me. I will be required to stretch a little further, to dig a little deeper at every stage of the journey. But for me, Islam has provided solid ground on which to build. The Salat (the five daily prayers) and *dhikr* (remembrance of Allah) are gifts which enable me to begin the process of polishing my heart clean of all the rust and grime which have prevented it from reflecting Light. Years of resistance, forgetfulness and rebellion had clogged up the conduit between me and my Lord. Salat and *dhikr* are the tools which make it possible to clear those blockages, allowing Healing, Power and Light to flow again.

I would never suggest that the authentic path is an easy one. Pain exists. Suffering is a reality. But reality can and does change. This is the paradox of powerlessness, as in the 'rock bottom' required before real recovery from addiction can begin. I can choose to perceive myself as a powerless victim, destined to a life of suffering and struggle, or I can take all the energy of that struggle, all the energy of the pain, and by my intention, my action and my submission to the God of the Wild Places, it can be transformed into something new, something which serves the world. A hundred and thirty miles across the Sahara is not easy. A hundred and fifteen miles through a Yukon winter is not easy. Divorce, redundancy, recovery from addiction, bereavement, whatever adversity a person faces in life, none of these things are easy, but if I open that conduit to the Lord of the worlds, however hard it gets, my soul will be nourished. Even in the darkest depths of the Yukon night I knew that somehow, I was meant to be there. I'd rather have this than the dissonant, gnawing feeling of emptiness, of betraying my own soul that I have often experienced in comfortable, warm, 'safe' surroundings, whatever the context. When I honour and feed the longing of my soul, I return nourished, with the ability to transform my perception of all aspects of my life.

Everything is in a constant process of change. I am created as part of an ever-changing, always renewed, ever-sustained universe. 'Everything perishes, except His face.'[17]

Conflict arises when I resist this change. In its desire to keep me 'safe' my ego wants to control everything and to maintain the status quo. It wants me to see this ever-changing universe as something which revolves around me, something separate. In this scenario I'm the only fixed point! Is it any surprise I get dizzy? When I take the risk and let go of this position, and let my heart and spirit guide me and step into the swirling, changing, ongoing, beautiful creation of which I am a part, then I can meet with my true nature, my true purpose. This is the 'Hero's Journey', the archetypal template, as true in microcosm as it

17   Qur'an, 28:88.

is in macrocosm. It is the seeker's journey from the 'base self', the 'soul which commands evil', through the 'blaming' soul, to the 'soul at peace': the 'perfected self'. Now that really is an adventure, the greatest journey through life.

For me it is also the drive to work in the morning when I'm gripped with irrational fears and anxieties about the day ahead. It is the journey from the armchair to the writing desk, and God knows that can be an expedition fraught with peril! It is any voyage through the stormy waters of resistance and fear. As I progress falteringly along my path, I am more and more convinced that, in some sense, I create my own reality. It may not be the whole story but on some level I make manifest the world around me, projecting outward what is going on inside me. I say this standing in all humility before the God of the Wild Places. The people, places and things that I meet along the way, especially those which generate strong reactions, mirror something of my own soul. If I am fearful, I will see danger everywhere. If I have a poverty-consciousness, I will bring scarcity into my life. If, on the other hand, I cultivate an attitude of abundance and faith in God's provision, and make this part of my belief system, then I will attract plenty.

It follows that I can either choose to be battered by the unpredictable seas of circumstance, or I can view my life through the lens of the Quest and embrace it with all my heart, submitting utterly to the God of the Wild Places. The degree to which I am able to submit, to let go and trust, seems to be the only factor limiting this extraordinary life-journey. In the early part of this story, I spoke about my shame and fear around financial matters. I related a time when I felt that my self-limiting perception of who I was had held me back and kept my world small. Much of my energy was spent in futile self-criticism and a litany of harsh self-judgements: I had 'missed the boat', I was destined to struggle along, living in a dingy rented flat for the rest of my life; I had failed to secure a decent home for my family. Trapped in this poverty-consciousness my potential remained largely untapped, and I was brought to the point of letting go.

I stood at the cliff's edge and took the liberating leap into the arms of my Higher Power. I realised that all of these judgements, this whole debating society inside my head, none of it was any of my business. What a revelation that was. The Real was the true source of my supply and would meet all my needs, spiritual, psychological, emotional and material, if I let Him.[18] My job was to believe that my God intended abundance and joy for me and to seek His purpose for my life. When I got out of my own way, things began to change. And to begin this journey I didn't even need any clear or fixed idea of who or what God was. Was It something outside, something inside, both? I really didn't know, and it didn't seem to matter. All I needed was a seed of belief.

'And if he draws near to Me an arm's length, I draw near to him a cubit, and if he draws near to Me a cubit, I draw near to him a fathom. And if he comes to Me walking, I go to him at speed.'[19]

---

18 This does not impose gender on God; words are inadequate in this context, and Islam also emphasises the feminine aspect of God. Gai Eaton, *Islam and the Destiny of Man* (Cambridge: Islamic Texts Society, 1994), p.83; William Chittick, *Divine Love: Islamic Literature and the Path to God* (New Haven and London: Yale University Press, 2013), p.26.

19 Hadith related by Bukhari, Muslim, al-Tirmidhi and Ibn Majah.

I did buy a little house: a modest but lovely home with a beautiful little garden full of birds. What's more, I have been freed from much of the anxiety which had held me frozen to the spot. I am now able to see and appreciate how blessed my life is. While I am not a Christian, I resonate with the message in the passage from the Christian scriptures: 'Seek ye first the kingdom of God and his righteousness and all these things shall be added unto you.' There are, of course, days (and weeks!) when I grab hold of the tiller, take control again and steer a course for the waters of fear and doubt. The difference is that I now know that when the darkness falls, which it inevitably will, the stars in the night sky will guide me back onto my true course.

When I really connect with my authentic purpose for being here, and single-mindedly and unreservedly accept that calling, it is then that the Universe moves to assist me. I confess that, with the notable exception of the call to the Wild Places outlined in these pages, I have only rarely had this single-minded clarity of vision, and then fleetingly. My experience has been that the benevolent trade-winds of inspiration seem to blow themselves out a few days into a voyage. The sail crumples and I find myself becalmed again. What do I do? I start rowing. I watch the horizon and pursue the wind. When I do this, it's never long before the sail billows and fills again and fair winds take me to where I need to be.

At times all I know is that I have to get my running shoes on, strap a weighted pack to my back and run until I'm drenched with sweat and my heart pounds against my ribcage. Sometimes my purpose really is as simple and direct as that, and it can bring a profound joy along with it. It's more than just the action of endorphins. The simple, trusting action creates a space into which inspiration can flow. At times when faced with some perplexing difficulty I may set out on a run because it's all I can do; but when the sweat starts to flow and I lock into the hypnotic rhythms of my breath, my heart and the motion of my limbs, I remember who I am. I remember the mission that has been entrusted to me. 'I nourish souls by showing glimpses of the God of the Wild Places.'

The machine, the rat-race far from nature, the grind created by a system that wants me to consume rather than create is not my reality. Working too hard to buy things I don't need is not my truth. I can choose to step out of the machine. My conscious intention can transform fear and negativity into blessing when I align it with my mission, the reason God put me on this earth. By my intention I can transform every journey, even the most mundane, into a pilgrimage. Each step becomes sacred; my life lived on what the First Nations people of North America call the Red Road; the *sirat al-mustaqim* (straight path) of Islam, living out my purpose. I must make the journey through life. The question is: will I accept the Call and be the hero in my own saga? Have I got what it takes to seek, find and claim the golden fleece, and then use it to bring healing to others?

I have come truly to believe that it is possible to move towards this reality. I did not have to accept the role assigned to me. It didn't fit. In truth, it was me who was holding on to that ill-fitting identity, that erroneous, limiting perception of who I was and what I was capable of. The anxieties and uncertainties of a rapidly-changing world have generated a corresponding spiritual hunger. I believe men need adventure, but without a sacred, transpersonal mission, without the spiritual 'jihad' against the ego, moving beyond self to the place of connection with all that is, no adventure will ever be enough in the ongoing search for soul. For me, the true source of my longing, though I didn't know it, was the Beloved, and it was in submission to the divine will in my life that I embarked upon the road of peace. I have a long way to travel on that road, with much to learn, but I have a deep sense that I am now facing the right way.

If I may speak directly, I earnestly encourage you to cut loose from what anchors you, to steer a course out of the harbour in which you shelter and risk the wild sea. Seek the unexplored continent of your purpose and, *in sha Allah*, it will find you. Give words to your mission and dare to live by those words. The world needs your gift; don't withhold it. The world needs heroes more than ever before.

Epilogue

WRITING THIS BOOK was a voyage in itself, one fraught with difficulty and strewn with obstacles. The seas were indeed stormy. I was nearly wrecked in the early stages of the writing journey when the clashing rocks of inexperience and impulsivity led to the loss of several months' work, work which I hadn't backed up. At one point I seemed to hit a solid rock wall. I had conflict at home, stress at work and I was completely stuck with my writing. I did something which I don't do often enough: midway through a particularly stressful and anxiety-fuelled morning in my place of work, I took myself off to a quiet place. I asked the God of the Wild Places to send me something, anything. I was feeling like a caged animal again. I was suffocating. An hour later, after a rapid and dramatic series of events, I was booked onto a flight to Greece, leaving the following day. I had been asked, at very short notice due to someone dropping out, to represent the charity I worked for on a fund-raising trek. The solid rock wall I'd hit turned out to be an opportunity to climb higher. Three days on from my prayer, after a soggy trudge through rain-drenched forest, a long, hot climb along a sun-bleached ridge above the treeline and a terrifying scramble up a spectacular, vertiginous, two-hundred metre rock pinnacle, I stood elated and joyful in the sun, on the summit of Mount Olympus, a Wild Place, home of the gods of myth. I surveyed a glorious panorama of mountain, forest and sea. And I felt that my heart would burst.

> '*The East and the West belong to God: Wherever you turn, there is His face.*'[20]

---

20 Qur'an 2:115.